BON

The L. Ron Hubbard Series

BRIDGE PUBLICATIONS, INC.
5600 E. Olympic Blvd.
Commerce, California 90022 USA

ISBN 978-1-4031-9881-5

Special acknowledgment is made to the L. Ron Hubbard Library for permission to reproduce photographs from his personal collection. Additional credits: pp. 1, 9, 37, 65, 79, 131, 145, 157, 179, 191, 217, back cover Topal/Shutterstock.com; p. 125 Justin Black/Shutterstock.com.

Printed in the United States of America

The L. Ron Hubbard Series: Photographer—English

The L. Ron Hubbard Series

PHOTOGRAPHER
WRITING
WITH LIGHT

Bridge

PUBLICATIONS, INC. ®

CONTENTS

Photographer: Writing with Light

An Introduction to L. Ron Hubbard | 1

First Frames | 9
    The Kodak Brownie Jr. | 11
    Guam | 17
    China | 29

Adventures and Expeditions | 37
    The Caribbean Motion Picture Expedition | 43
    The Puerto Rican Mineralogical Expedition | 47
    Voyage to Alaska | 51
    Stereo Photography | 53

Photographs from the Formative Years of Scientology | 65
    Greece | 72
    The Canon | 72

New Photographic Vistas from Saint Hill | 79
    The Rolleiflex Collection | 89
    The Saint Hill Darkroom | 91
    The Rear Screen Projector | 95
    Letter to Professor Land | 99
    Sir Robert Fossett's Circus | 104
    Selections for Exhibition | 109
    The Deardorff | 115
    Self-Portraits | 117
    The Linhof | 121

Is It Art? *by L. Ron Hubbard* | 125

A Photographic Holiday | 131
　Nikonos Underwater Camera | 135
　The Voigtländer | 136
　Flamenco Dancers | 139
　The Bullfight | 141

Ports of Call | 145
　The Rollei 35 | 146
　The Gandolfi | 151
　Mamiya C33 | 153

The Photo Shoot Organization | 157
　Cameras of the Photo Shoot Organization | 160
　The Lisbon Maritime Museum | 163
　The Synagogue of Mikvé Israel–Emanuel | 167
　On Behalf of the New York Explorers Club | 171
　The Curaçao Bridge | 172
　Portrait of a Caribbean Minister | 175

Filters | 179
　Color Temperature | 181
　The SEI (Salford Electrical Instruments) Meter | 184

The Latter Years | 191

    The Minox | 192

    Minolta CLE | 193

    Gadget Bag | 196

    The 35mm Systems | 202

    Leica | 204

    The Camera Room | 206

    Testing | 212

Instruction | 217

    Notes on Composition *by L. Ron Hubbard* | 221

    Camera Stable Data *by L. Ron Hubbard* | 223

One Last Image | 227

Appendix

    Glossary | 231

    Index | 259

An Introduction to
L. Ron Hubbard

Photography, as L. Ron Hubbard reminds us, means light writing—literally, *photo* (light) and *graphy* (writing)—and given all he provided in the name of photographic communication, that definition is particularly apt.

Presented here are photographs, essays, anecdotes and notes from some sixty years of writing with light. As contents will suggest, those years were extraordinarily rich and diverse. A seasoned traveler in his youth, Ron had logged more than a quarter of a million miles by the age of nineteen, twice crossing the Pacific to a rarely glimpsed Asia. Returning to the United States in 1929 (and while still a student at George Washington University), he was alternately seen barnstorming across America's hinterland and heading an expedition into the Caribbean. Upon leaving the university in 1932, he soon set out again for Puerto Rico where he headed the island's first complete mineralogical survey under American protectorship. Then followed his 1940 Alaskan voyage to rechart a British Columbian and Alaskan coastline, and his various European, African and Caribbean travels through the 1960s and 1970s. The point: when speaking of L. Ron Hubbard as photographer, we are speaking of light writing far and wide.

The second point bearing mention from the outset is the LRH dedication to technical excellence. For only with a mastery of photographic fundamentals and equipment, Ron tells us, can one achieve full freedom of photographic expression. How is a particular film best exposed, processed and printed? What are the strengths of a particular camera or the

Left
With Graflex,
Saint Hill,
England, 1965

Left With Linhof, Saint Hill grounds, England, 1965

relative weakness of a particular lens? How does one most effectively measure and utilize light, whether natural or artificial, and what best determines the arrangement of a scene? These were the questions every professional asked. While even in this digital age, these remain the fundamental questions of the art form. In reply, then, came intense LRH study, refinement and codification. Indeed, from shutter click to final print, he finally left nothing to chance—framing and composition, focus and exposure, developing and printing—all utterly nailed with astonishing precision, and with a range of equipment that is equally astonishing. Moreover, and given technical advancements since his first 1924 snapshots, "I've had to learn photography four times completely from scratch."

But what he learned, he willingly shared. And therein lies our third and perhaps most important introductory point: from those sixty years of professional photography came all Ron supplied for the benefit of anyone who would similarly write with light. To briefly cite but a few examples: For the budding photographer, so frequently daunted by complex theory and technicalities, Ron offered his checklisted distillation of just what comprises any perfect

> "...an LRH photograph provides us with a glimpse of how Ron viewed this world."

photograph and thus a means by which even the beginner might immediately elevate snapshots to full *quality* pictures. From his philosophic examination of photographic composition came a fully *workable* definition of the well-composed shot—or, for that matter, any visual presentation. Then again, from his analysis of the perfect negative came his benchmark procedures for the testing of film speeds and equipment, his novel employment of light meters and filters—and all of it carefully delineated in several hundred pages of instructional essays.

So yes, the commitment was considerable and lifelong. And if an LRH photograph provides us with a glimpse of how Ron viewed this world, that commitment provides even more on the man himself. For example, quite apart from candid work and an expertise with early (and then notoriously temperamental) color film, Ron's photographic forte was action. In consequence, and in addition to the rodeos, air meets and motorcycle races, we shall follow Ron into a Las Palmas bullring for shots of "spills and tosses and trammelings galore." We shall further venture through infamously treacherous seas for a photographic record of uncharted coasts, climb into biplane cockpits for literally hair-raising shots at five thousand feet, and enter a snarling lion's cage to record the big cats at work. Finally—and if somewhat less adventurous, but certainly no less telling—we shall peer into a darkroom on the island of Guam where he first honed skills of film development and retouching in 1927, at the age of sixteen, ascend windblown ramparts barely a year later for his celebrated series of China's Great Wall, and follow his gaze across Saint Hill downs for his equally celebrated southern English landscapes through the 1960s.

There is more: While many a reader may have heard tell of LRH shoots for a British circus, a Caribbean tourist board or a Portuguese maritime museum, here are stories from those shoots. Here is Ron with ringmaster Sir Robert Fossett providing publicity shots (from some four hundred frames, as a matter of fact) to finally fill that big top to capacity. Here he is again with rabbis of the New World's oldest synagogue and afloat in a Lisbon estuary to capture a floating replica of Vasco da Gama's flagship. And if every LRH photograph is itself a story, so, too, is every LRH camera. Consequently, and to cite but three from that astonishing array of dozens: here is the Linhof with which he shot his famously familiar self-portraits (on traditional glass negatives, no less), here is the much-loved Rolleiflex batting off shots "faster than scat," and here is the first color-shooting Polaroid Land Camera, inspiring correspondence with Professor Land himself.

As noted, LRH photographs presented here have been selected from the full breadth

of Ron's long and expansive career or from an LRH photographic library comprising tens of thousands of images. In addition to selections from L. Ron Hubbard photographic calendars and the definitive *L. Ron Hubbard: Images of a Lifetime—A Photographic Biography,* we offer many a previously unpublished print.

We further offer a sampling from the larger body of LRH instructional essays, also never broadly seen, as well as rare LRH comments on

"...from those sixty years of professional photography came all Ron supplied for the benefit of anyone who would similarly write with light."

cameras and equipment, and still more again on the greater perspective from a lifetime of writing with light. ■

On Puget Sound, near Camp Parsons, Washington, 1925

FIRST FRAMES

First Frames

BEYOND A FEW STATIONARY YEARS IN HIS BOYHOOD HOME of Helena, Montana, L. Ron Hubbard's youth was marked by much precipitous travel in the wake of his father's naval career. Although he would eventually see many a far-flung and fascinating land, the loneliness of impermanence was undeniable. Schoolmates were transitory,

friendships temporary and as Ron so touchingly phrased it, "Each time I came HOME I was different, HOME was different and as though making a V in time, HOME and I diverged, wider and wider."

At about the age of seven, however, and as if to form a more lasting perspective, Ron acquired a camera—an unnamed wooden box camera, probably a gift from his grandfather. Shortly thereafter, he acquired the Kodak Brownie Jr., mass-produced, with a string-set shutter, but remarkably modern in several respects. As a first introductory note to what ensued, let us describe photography of 1918, as still a complex infant, or at least a trying adolescent. The first flexible negative film, for example, and thus the technical basis of Ron's Kodak, had only appeared some twenty years earlier, while shutter speed was still generally fixed at a relatively slow 1/25th of a second. Then, too, and while many a snapshot graced mantels of American homes, the truly quality photograph remained a fairly esoteric subject.

The Hubbard family home was typical. While Ron's seafaring father regularly packed a camera, his efforts were modest—primarily casual shots of shipmates or ports of call, and a somewhat formal portrait of a Captain S. V. Graham, snapped "with his permission." Also found within the Harry Ross Hubbard portfolio are stock shots of muzzle blasts from battleship guns, seascapes of vessels on maneuver and a rescue of "nine men, nine women, baby and goat."

To best introduce Ron's pursuit of the subject, then, we best turn to his own 1924 account of a first photographic lesson and the tribulations of testing for a Boy Scout Photography Merit Badge. The setting was Washington, DC,

With an early Kodak Brownie Jr., San Diego, California, 1919

The Kodak Brownie Jr.

The original point-and-shoot, and initially selling for just one dollar, the Kodak Brownie Jr. probably accomplished more for the popularization of photography than any camera in history. A linear descendant of the original factory-loaded Kodak box, Ron's 1916–1927 No. 2C Autographic Kodak Jr. proved especially popular as among the first to carry roll film (as opposed to the cumbersome and slow-loading single film sheets or glass negatives of earlier-generation cameras). If otherwise not particularly rare or fine, here was nonetheless Ron's first cherished camera, and he kept it in fine working order for the better part of sixty years. ∎

Left With Kodak Brownie Jr., Montana, 1924

where he would soon gain renown as the nation's youngest Eagle Scout. Although not specifically mentioned, candidates for that photographic badge were required to not only demonstrate competence with the camera, but the fundamentals of darkroom development. Also pertinent are later LRH comments on the difference between constructive criticism and "invalidative criticism," with the all-too-prevalent latter so frequently based upon nothing more than mere opinions of "authority." Otherwise, Ron's diary entry tells all:

"I cast about for another badge and decided on 'Photography.' Down to the National Museum I went to see the examiner of that merit badge.

"He sat at a big desk in a room that was cluttered with human skulls and proceeded to inform me that I knew nothing about photography. I agreed with him perfectly and came again another day to find the same verdict. A month and ten visits later he signed my card just to be rid of me, telling me that I'd never know anything about photography due to my exceptional stupidity. This is rather abated by the fact that I just sold six pictures to the *National Geographic* magazine."

Yet even prior to that first crucial sale, and with the merit badge still newly sewn to his sleeve, came a number of other LRH photographs to abate that examiner's verdict. His focus primarily lay on scouting trails—or such adjacent attractions as the Lincoln Memorial. With his

passage to Washington State's Camp Parsons, shots included fellow scouts, scoutmasters and auxiliary staff. Then again, with a return to Montana came still further study with Western naturalist/portraitist William Taylor. But in either case, and as specifically underscored by his sale to the *National Geographic,* the LRH field of focus would soon quite dramatically broaden.

Guam

Ron's first South Pacific crossing commenced in 1927 with a circuitous voyage to the island of Guam. Next, following a return to Montana through the winter and spring of 1928, he again set out for the Marianas en route to the Chinese mainland. Those familiar with the larger LRH story will recall these travels as regards his greater trail of research to Dianetics and Scientology—with his sifting through "airy spiralings and dread mysteries" of primitive societies, his deeper search for a seemingly inscrutable riddle of existence and a final realization that where one indeed found real pockets of wisdom, "it was carefully hidden and given out only as superstition." In such terms, these photographs comprise a visual record of that search and actually show us what he saw.

By the same token, however, there is much to say in purely photographic terms. Described as an American territory of small extent, and then serving as the principal fueling station for a United States Asiatic Fleet, Guam was not as unlikely a site of photographic advancement as one might imagine. For just as Harry Ross Hubbard avidly collected snapshots of ports and shipmates, so, too, did fellow seamen. In consequence, the island's Mayhew photo studio thrived.

The proprietor was an Anglo-gone-somewhat-native. With sons approximately Ron's age, the LRH-Mayhew arrangement was a natural. Ron served as darkroom apprentice, and "quite religiously" so, while Mayhew supervised and instructed. For a sense of the duties, Ron tells of manning developing trays as Mayhew fed in prints with a tong-paddle—timing by instinct and eye, then flipping prints into the next tray like pancakes. "A standard professional line," Ron dubbed it, and similarly described processing and enlarging in the same assembly-line fashion. Indeed, only Mrs. Mayhew's laborious hand coloring of black and white photographs could not be subjected to systemized production. But in either case, Ron would reference that Mayhew studio as a steppingstone to professional realms, and especially so in terms of standardization and an ever-vigilant eye for potential error, e.g., given tropical humidity, film shot on the

Above "Swimming in the Namo River in Agat, Guam. Saturday night comes every day to the Chamorro child. While their mothers are about the daily washing, these children find ample amusement in the stream. One garment is required by law to be worn but that of the boatman is probably in the wash."—LRH. Purchased by *National Geographic*, 1930

Left "Sunday Sunset, Guam"—LRH

"A hand-hewn ifil log in the jungles, Guam. This is a native wood of the island, much harder than mahogany. It is so heavy that it will not float. It defies the ravages of time and insects and turns black in the course of a hundred years."—LRH. Purchased by *National Geographic,* 1930

Above "A street in Merizo, Guam. This Chamorro farmer is on his way from his village home to his ranch. The heavy wheels of the cart are built of solid ifil wood. The carabao is guided by a ring in the nose to which is attached a single rope."—LRH. Purchased by *National Geographic*, 1930

Right "The carabao takes a refreshing siesta after the day's toil."—LRH

island was particularly subject to spotting and best processed quickly. He would also speak of these days for what he gleaned as regards practical technique and technical possibilities—as when utilizing paper cutouts to re-create battle panoramas, or his superimposed self-portraits amidst seemingly enormous insects. Then again, here was the studio where he first explored techniques of double exposure and his own hand tinting of black and white.

Yet the real focus, and most memorable vista, lay with the island itself. After all, it was then and there he first broke into professional ranks with the sale of photographs to America's then premier photographic publication, *National Geographic*. Reprinted here with explanatory LRH notes, the shots followed from his truly exhaustive exploration of the island—quite literally from subterranean caves to the cliff-top ruins of a Spanish fortress. As photographs suggest, he further delved quite deeply into an insular native Chamorro culture, and so provided precisely the stuff for which *National Geographic* remains famous to this day.

Sunset Guam, M.I.

"The natives play a queer instrument
called a billibutugun"—LRH

"Sunset,
Guam,
M. I."
[Mariana
Islands]
—LRH

"A great underground stream is the source of
a great deal of wonder"—LRH

"Sunrise at Piti
7/18/27"—LRH

"Beach at Tumon, Guam"—LRH

"Don't be frightened kiddies
you'd look as fierce as this carabao too,
if *you* had to live in Guam"—LRH

"Clothes Pounders"—LRH

"Jesus displays a local product"—LRH

"Fishermen's huts bordering the lagoon, San Antonio, Guam. Made of ifil wood, these huts have sheltered many generations. The thatch roofs are made of nipa fronds which must be renewed every three years. The Chamorro girls have just spread their washing on the racks in the foreground."—LRH. Purchased by *National Geographic*, 1930

China

JUST AS GUAM PROVED SIGNIFICANT philosophically *and* photographically, so, too, China. As noted, Ron twice ventured into a then somewhat forbidden China—first into Shanghai and Hong Kong, then deeper still into Peking and Mongolia. Given he packed a light trunk, equipment was minimal. In fact, he worked with a preloaded rental camera and a then popular Agfa foldout, most probably acquired from a Young Photo Company along Shanghai's famously colorful Nanking Road.

Among other notes on technique and approach, he describes his specialty as harbor panoramas with plying junks, and candids from the streets. As a word on the former, he speaks of stepping to the railing of a passenger liner for a twilight shot of the backlit schooner aboard which he had sailed from Guam. As a word on that candid work, he alludes to a local fear of cameras and popular beliefs that photographers might actually snatch a man's soul. In consequence, one had to shoot quickly and unobtrusively (a particular challenge with film of the day). He also provides a few choice comments on

what those shots reflected, as in: "Money has depreciated as to food but remained the same as to wage, creating a starved condition around the coolie..."

Rightfully eliciting the most commentary, however, was Ron's celebrated Great Wall series. Dating from two centuries before the birth of Christ, and 1,500 miles in length, the wall is factually the largest structure ever reared by Man. Construction consumed decades, countless lives and earned a Chinese epitaph as "the ruin of one generation" for "the salvation of many." While guidebooks of Ron's day advertised a fifteen-minute walk to the wall, the higher ramparts—and thus the truly grand vista—required much more. In fact, he tells of first convincing a native conductor to bring a Peking-bound train to an unscheduled stop below the Nan-k'ou Pass, and only then commencing an hour-long climb to the ramparts. Results, nonetheless, proved plainly worth the effort. Indeed, Ron was among the first to capture a full seven turns of the wall in quite dramatic contrast to typically dreary views of but twenty or thirty feet. The point, as

Above
An unobtrusive candid of life in China, 1928

Left Mariana Maru at twilight, China Sea, 1928

he later explained: "The way the thing twists and turns, it appears that there are dozens of walls instead of one." The greater point: he soon enjoyed a second crucial sale—this time to a famed stock-house agency of Underwood & Underwood, where arrangements soon led to the publication of those China Wall shots in various geography texts of the day. ■

Above
China's Great Wall, near Nan-k'ou Pass, 1928

Left Wang Po River, Shanghai, China, 1927

Seven turns of the Great Wall from above Nan-k'ou Pass, China, 1928

Experimental Aircraft, San Diego, California, 1934

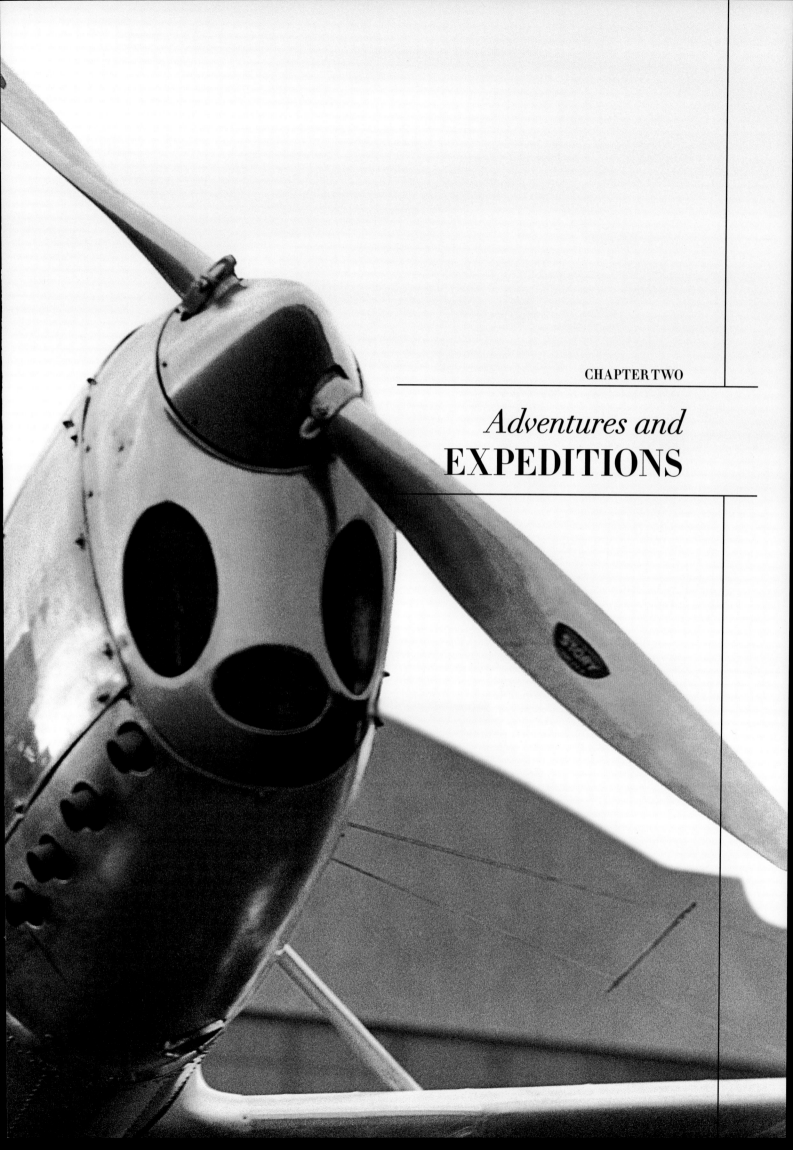

CHAPTER TWO

Adventures and
EXPEDITIONS

Adventures and
Expeditions

HAVING LEGITIMATELY ENTERED PROFESSIONAL RANKS with the sale of shots from abroad, Ron continued along an equally professional vein upon his 1929 return to Washington, DC. As we have said, his forte was action and he would literally pursue that action across rough lands, high seas and blustery skies.

Initially, though—and however improbable for a young man late of the China Wall ramparts—he found himself in pursuit of shots for the society page. The circumstances were classic: With portfolio in hand, he landed a freelance spot on a then prestigious *Washington Herald.* Assignments were typically varied and catch as catch can. He photographed prominent military mascots, including an admiral's terrier. He authored and supplied the shots for what amounted to a front-page photographic essay on the dismantling of a much-loved trolley line. (Also included was a particularly nostalgic look at the horse-drawn origins of that trolley to, all in all, inspire 283 mournful letters to the editor.) Finally—and here we must envision a city-suited Ron with press card in the hatband of a Stetson—he wandered the

bridle paths of Washington's Rock Creek Park to photograph such equestrian debutantes as Secretary of State, Henry Stimson's daughter. He further speaks of halting society ladies on ballroom steps, and otherwise working one end of the city to another for photographs that ultimately earned larger checks than even five or ten thousand written words.

More to the point of these years, and rather more fitting, are photographs to follow here: adventures and expeditions. Himself the feature of newspaper articles as a free-flight daredevil and barnstormer, Ron quite naturally qualified to shoot and write for *The Sportsman Pilot.* Then the bible of private aviators, the publication reflected what amounted to a national craze in the wake of Lindbergh's transatlantic flight. The focus was precisely what Ron supplied: profiles of such

Ron (on wing), with aerial photography camera, Port Huron, Michigan, 1931

concerning the loss of alternative technologies in the wake of specialization.)

Additionally on behalf of *The Sportsman Pilot* came Ron's aerial shoot of Charlemagne's Haitian fortress (Citadelle Laferrière). Conducted for a 1934 article entitled "West Indies Whys and Whithers," and describing a Caribbean island-hopping flight from Florida to Martinique, the shoot proved a story in itself. "You'll hit plenty of nasty little squalls which bounce you around like a hat in a hurricane," Ron reported, and elsewhere described shooting from his knees in the open rear cockpit of a two-seater biplane, i.e., unfastening the seatbelt, leaning out to clear the fuselage from the camera frame, then firing very quickly before a two-G drop left one all but suspended in midair.

The all-embracing point: one learned to *see* a picture, *compose* a picture, focus, shoot and reload very quickly—and particularly so given equipment of the day. Indeed, Ron most generally employed the classic pressman's Graflex, accommodating but a single sheet of 4 × 5 inch film or, at best, a slow loading pack of five sheets. In either case, that Graflex was a far cry from the motor-driven, fully automatic camera of today's photojournalist, who regularly bats off five frames a second. In other words, and even under less challenging circumstances, shots

aerial luminaries as *Spirit of St. Louis* designer T. Claude Ryan and his experimental Ryan ST, or coverage of such significant meets as the Langley Day race and beanbag bombing competition at Washington's College Park Airfield. (Of additional interest at that College Park airstrip were Ron's photograph of, and interview with, pioneering aviator E. H. Young—lone proponent of thirteen lost methods for heavier-than-air flight, and so later remarked upon in LRH lectures

Right The Graflex

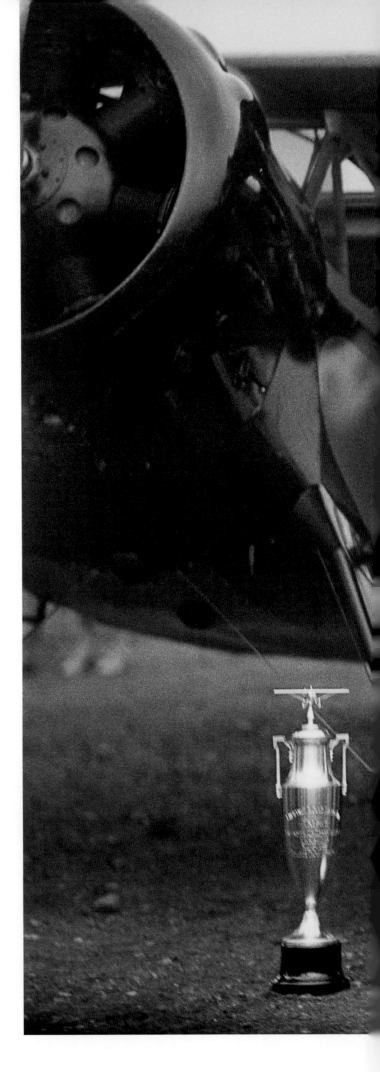

were fleeting and equipment allowed for but one photographic opportunity. Consequently, the professional gained a truly rare dexterity, with instant recognition of a picture and commensurately fast focusing, framing, shooting and reloading of that single film sheet. Or as Ron later remarked: one learned to operate a camera "standing on your head."

The Caribbean Motion Picture Expedition

NOTWITHSTANDING THE IMPLICATION of a Caribbean Motion Picture Expedition, the venture is best remembered from the stills. All commenced in the spring of 1932, with notices soliciting a few hearty collegians for a voyage to pirate haunts aboard one of the last of the four-masted schooners, remembered today as the *Doris Hamlin*. What ensued (and is fully chronicled in *The L. Ron Hubbard Series: Adventurer/Explorer*) was as rousing an adventure as any young man of the day might have hoped for—with sail-shredding winds off a Puerto Rican coast, encounters with barracuda in the Sargasso Sea and a glimpse in the mouth of an active Martinique volcano.

If the photographic footnotes were somewhat less dramatic, those notes are nonetheless illuminating. For example, among other letters of the day, one finds an LRH exchange with one Edward Groth from rarefied Kodak research laboratories where tropical incubators subjected film to precisely those steamy Caribbean climes. Specifically under discussion were ways and means of preserving negatives in ultrahigh humidity. (Ice "only tends to condense the water vapor...and form minute water droplets," advised Groth, while roll film proved particularly susceptible to droplet damage. But in any case he added: "It's quite a treat to find someone with practical experience on tropical film conditions.") Eventually in reply to such questions, Ron enlisted a Mr. Bush and Mr. Edwards—also from Kodak, but said to "know more about tropical film conditions than anyone else in the world"—to advise on field developing procedures. The point—and a consistent thread through these formative photographic years—Ron was continually pushing technical limits and so searching out the one or two consummate specialists who similarly "knew more than anyone else in the world."

If duties as expedition leader generally kept Ron from his Graflex, his tropical film research still proved well worth the effort. Indeed, expedition cameramen finally sold shots to both a Baltimore syndication house and the *New York Times*.

Left The *Doris Hamlin*, Baltimore, Maryland, 1932

The *Doris Hamlin,* en route to Martinique, 1932

The Puerto Rican Mineralogical Expedition

"*Up to my waist in water. Squishy in my boots. Sweat in my eyes... The sun beating down between two high, wind-breaking creek banks. The Graflex is going out to the diggin's tomorrow.*"—LRH, 12 November 1932

Specifically, that Graflex was to document the digging of a first test sluice in a Puerto Rican hinterland and mineral specimens collected from adjacent mines. Also of photographic interest were the highland trails along which Ron conducted that island's first complete mineralogical survey under United States protectorship, and the cliffs of Palo Blanco where Conquistadores first launched "this West Indian gold crusade."

While Ron himself chronicled that legendary adventure in "A Sample Pick Saga" (see *The L. Ron Hubbard Series: Adventurer/Explorer*), the photographic record of his 1933 Puerto Rican Mineralogical Expedition provides yet another interesting subtext. "I had my camera in one hand and the reins in the other," he wrote from a flyblown shack in Corozal on the heels of a day spent astride an "ugly little stallion." Apparently intended to illustrate newspaper features on that futile and "mad lust of man for gold," shots included swollen rivers, abandoned shafts, tortuous trails and distant smoke from native fires. If his eventual discovery of silicon and manganese deposits finally kept Ron from the typewriter—at least temporarily—the challenge of field photography was not soon forgotten. Merely, he would exchange that little stallion's reins for the tiller of a thirty-two-foot ketch.

Above
The Palo Blanco region first mined by the Spaniards in the 1600s

Left Mouth of an abandoned mine shaft in the Puerto Rican hinterland, 1932

Testing a sluicing chute, Puerto Rico, 1932

Voyage to Alaska

DUBBED THE ALASKAN RADIO Experimental Expedition and conducted on behalf of a United States Hydrographic Office and beneath the famed New York Explorers Club flag, Ron's fifteen-hundred-mile voyage from Puget Sound to the Alaskan Panhandle is similarly the stuff of legend. Moreover, if his passage through British Columbia's treacherous inland waterways has been amply talked about, the photographic record is just as illuminating.

Primarily intended to augment navigational corrections of existing charts, his camera was a Leica IIIb—borrowed from a friend and fitted with what was termed a Stereoly lens mount for producing stereo-optic images. The essential design, pioneered by Austrian topographers, provided a three-dimensional view for mapping directly from photographs. In all, Ron managed some four hundred frames of previously mischarted coastlines and entirely misplaced islands. While for a sense of the actual shoots one need only peruse those logs telling of millrace tides and "heart in the throat navigation." Then, too, we hear of Ron passing that Leica to a first mate, literally lashed to the mast.

With his landing in the southern Alaskan port of Ketchikan, the photographic record took another turn entirely: specifically for what Ron envisioned as a formally published account of life along a fading frontier. While the Second World War finally left the project shelved, the album remains—complete with LRH captions and filled with shots of fisherfolk, tradesmen and general roustabouts.

Left
Landfall in Ketchikan, Alaska, 1940

Below
The Stereoly lens mounted on the Leica IIIb produced a stereo image, providing a three-dimensional view for mapping

Stereo or Double-image Photograph

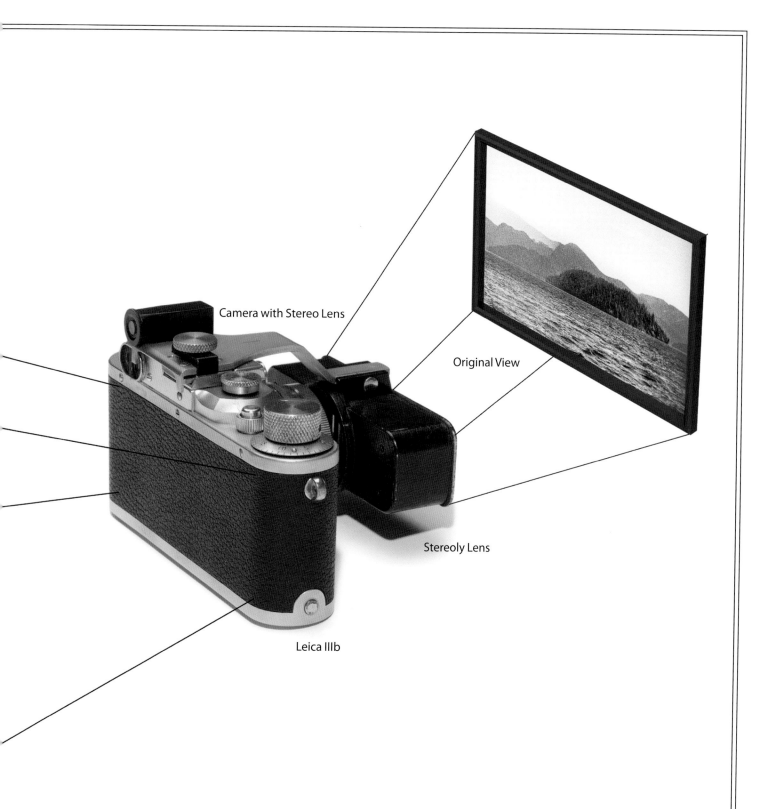

Camera with Stereo Lens

Original View

Stereoly Lens

Leica IIIb

Stereo Photography

A Leica IIIb, fitted with a Stereoly lens, shoots a stereo or double-image photograph. This photograph, when viewed through a stereo projector or viewer, produces a three-dimensional image to assist topographers in mapping directly from photographs. ■

A town of notorious lanes, an infamous brothel and genuinely murderous taverns, Ketchikan was nothing if not dangerously colorful. In illustration, Ron speaks of the shotgunned bodies regularly pulled from the straits—unless swept out past Cape Chacon—at which point, as he quipped: "Nobody ever knows anything more about it." By the same token, however, residents of the Panhandle were quite famously friendly, and particularly to renowned author and master mariner L. Ron Hubbard. After all, here was a bona fide local hero arriving beneath an Explorers Club flag to both entertain as a balladeer and answer nautical questions on radio station KGBU. Then, too, here was a clearly consummate photographer very much involved with his subjects. ▪

Left
"These reaches and passages are long, narrow passes, wild and deep and straight"—LRH en route to Alaska, 1940

"A KGBU ANNOUNCER running the Sears request program. Requests are hurled out in batches of thirty and then a record is played. Alaska, having a thin-spread populace, uses the request program to the limit."—LRH

"GAMBLING is wide-open business in Alaska, constituting a major industry. Here we have a full house, a straight flush and two pairs, the last belonging to a 'cheechalker' [a tenderfoot or newcomer] whose back is to the camera and has no mother to guide him."—LRH

"JIMMY BRITTON, the owner of KGBU is his own radio engineer, .9 of the announcing staff, program director, advertising salesman, business manager, staff writer, news commentator and legal staff of his station, though KGBU is the 'Voice of Alaska' and covers half a million square miles as the only contact of Alaska with the outside world. Inability to get men rather than shortage of business makes Jimmy work much harder than his plump figure would indicate."—LRH

"THOMAS BASIN with an Alaska steam vessel in Tongass Narrows, beyond. The small fishing vessels whose masts reach up into this rainy day are, to a large number, radio equipped and skippered by fishermen who have made the personal acquaintance of all the rocks of these dangerous shores. Because of their mine-carrying capacity and the lack of pilots for larger boats, these make ideal patrol vessels in these sheltered waters. The organization of two hundred of them into an Alaskan patrol would serve better than two hundred destroyers or MTBs [Motor Torpedo Boats]."—LRH

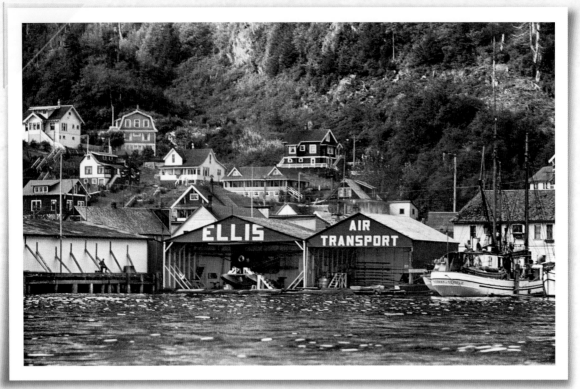

"PLANES in Alaska 'use a brush hook' to get over the ridges, so low is the weather. Ellis is one of the pioneers of flying and runs a weekly 'Klawock Clipper' to the 'West Coast,' a district in the islands west of SE Alaska."—LRH

"THE MAGICIAN attended by the motor launch, STOOGE, an inboard boat 16' in length which pursues the old master astern through wave, wind and fog, always ready in case the uncharted rocks and reefs may take their toll of the old master's bows and bottom."—LRH

"GAFFED SALMON, taken by Indian boys from Fish Creek which runs through the center of Ketchikan. Fish Creek, the ruby bulb district is said to be the only place in the world 'where the fish and the fishermen come to spawn.' These salmon weigh from twenty to forty pounds apiece."—LRH

"GAFFING SALMON from the bridge at Fish Creek. Indian boys, with a hook on the end of a pole, spear the fish from the swimming thousands. The hook, springing free, becomes a gaff and the fish are hauled in by means of a line attached to the pole. The work is bloody because so many fish get away, though badly ripped."—LRH

"JACK O'DONNELL, huge, jovial and red-bearded, wonders if he really does want the rest of this beer or why he began to drink beer in the first place. His wife Gertrude follows Jack's many adventures with rare aplomb. Jack has been blown up, drowned, shipwrecked, broke, rich and drunk."—LRH

"INDIANS IN ALASKA have the same allergy to whiskey possessed by those of the US. This is the beginning of a war which, a little later, cleaned out the saloon. The lights went out with the first blow, handed over by the thin fellow who is here engaged in tracing the ancestry of the seated Indian and finding that it led swiftly into 'floaters' and other such things. He may be right. These are typical Tlingit faces."—LRH

"AN INDUSTRY of major importance runs full blast to the merry tune this barkeep is playing upon his cash register. In a town of five thousand people there are sixty-one saloons."—LRH

Ron's "portrait by candlelight" on the birthday of his Alaskan Expedition deckhand

A few blocks from Ron's home in Kensington, London, England, circa 1957

CHAPTER THREE

Photographs from the
FORMATIVE YEARS OF SCIENTOLOGY

Photographs from the
Formative Years of Scientology

WHILE L. RON HUBBARD AND SCIENTOLOGY WILL forever remain linked in the public mind, few realize that many a photograph chronicling both the growth and scope of a burgeoning Scientology was, in fact, an LRH photograph. Then, too—and even more to the point of photographs presented here—were

Ron's far-flung shoots of all lands he visited while personally attending to the worldwide Scientology growth.

For the fully classic example, consider his March 1961 Acropolis shoot from an Athens layover to newly formed Scientology offices in Johannesburg. Between lectures to Greek physicians (on Scientology assists for the ailing) and procedural advice to local Scientology ministers, Ron writes of scaling "a few hills" to "shoot perhaps 150 pictures of ruins." Also noted, selections from those 150 pictures would eventually see publication in *The Auditor* magazine and so illustrate an LRH essay on Scientology's philosophic roots. Similarly, between administrative duties in rapidly expanding London offices and lectures on Scientology auditing techniques (including, incidentally, techniques for the rehabilitation

of artistic skills), he writes of shooting a "very exciting" and "very sociable" London. Or even more specifically: "Sort of a New York of 1890, but much, much faster with its streets jammed with fast small cars, huge fast buses."

While his camera of choice for portraits of Scientology staff remained the Graflex, letters from late 1955 also allude to a then novel single-lens Reflex-Korelle. Then again—and more on the matter later—one finds a first exchange of correspondence with the Polaroid Corporation concerning Ron's testing of an equally novel Polaroid Land Camera. Finally, even if incidentally, there was Ron's gift to his father of an especially fine Rolleicord, and Ron's jocular reply to his father's selection of first shots, "That camera of yours shoots pictures twice or ten times as good as any other Rollei I've seen. Of course it couldn't be the photographer!"

Old Brompton Road, London, England, 1956

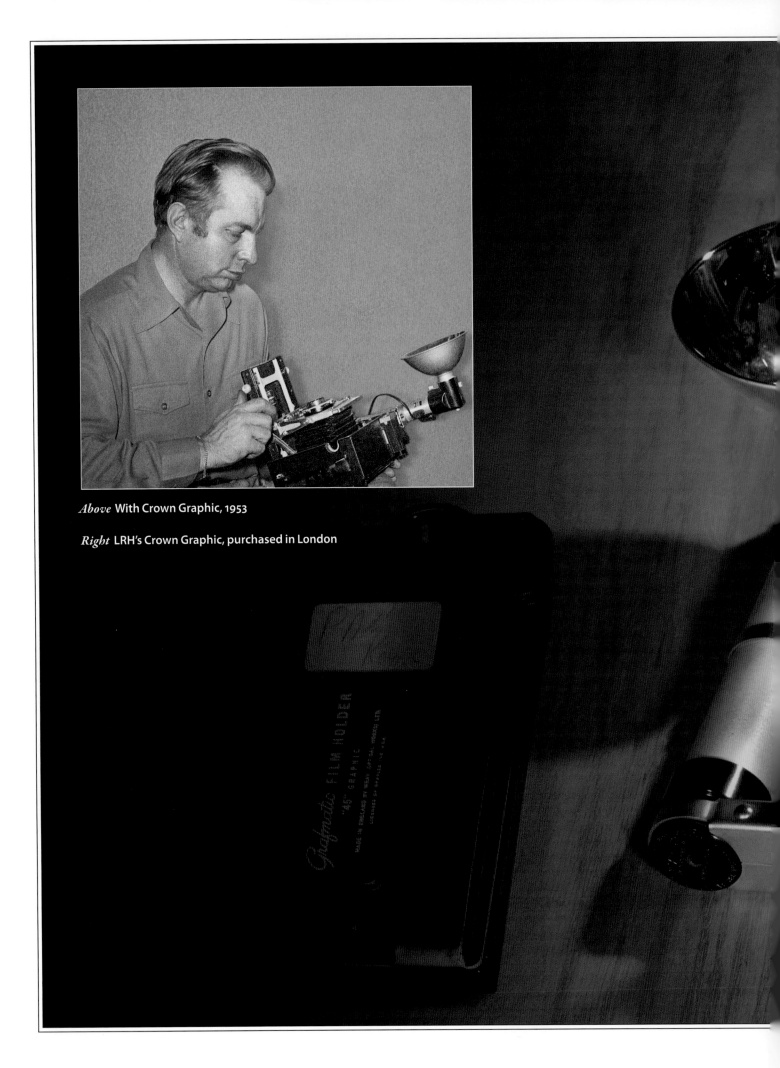

Above With Crown Graphic, 1953

Right LRH's Crown Graphic, purchased in London

Above
Old Brompton
Road, London,
England, 1956

Right
Earls Court Road,
London, England,
circa 1956

More typically, however, were remarks on methods and technique: "I am having the most luck with available light photography," he remarked, i.e., natural or usual light, as in sunlight and lamplight. Then followed his summary conclusions from tests of film designed for low-light use—tests specifically conducted under challengingly dim chandeliers of a west London auditorium before shoots of a post-lecture party. Also of concern were methods of actually incorporating those shots into an *Ability* magazine or a *Journal of Scientology*—which, by turns, sparked many an involved discussion on methods of processing, printing reproduction and mimeographing. The underlying point, however, is altogether less complex: while publications illustrating Scientology's growth through the formative decade beyond 1952 may have finally reached several million readers, what pictorially fueled those publications was a relatively unseen L. Ron Hubbard camera. ▪

Fox-hunting dogs, East Grinstead, England, circa 1963

Greece

Above With Canon, Athens, 1961

The Canon

During a six-day stay and in between lectures to Greek physicians and Scientology parishioners in 1961, Ron scaled "a few hills" to shoot some 150 photographs of the Acropolis. Selections from these 150 photos would later appear in *The Auditor* magazine to illustrate an LRH essay on Scientology's philosophic roots. ■

Right The Parthenon, atop the Acropolis, Athens, 1961

The Acropolis, Athens, 1961

Saint Hill grounds, East Grinstead, England, 1965

CHAPTER FOUR

New Photographic
VISTAS FROM SAINT HILL

New Photographic Vistas from Saint Hill

IF WE SHALL ALWAYS REMEMBER SAINT HILL MANOR AS L. Ron Hubbard's home, then those memories are most indelibly fixed from his photographs of the era. All effectively commenced in late 1961, when "incautiously and in a moment of weakness," he enrolled on a New York Institute of Photography correspondence course. Founded in 1910,

and described as the oldest and largest photographic school, the Institute legitimately boasts of having trained more professionals than any commensurate school. (Among other illustrious alumni, for example, is famed *Life* magazine photo-essayist Eugene Smith.) Lessons are provided on all photographic fundamentals, with specialized supplements in portraiture, fashion, advertising and more. Those familiar with the larger body of L. Ron Hubbard works may additionally recall the course *vis-à-vis* Ron's development of tools for literacy and learning—collectively known as Study Technology, and presently at work in many thousands of classrooms world over (see *The L. Ron Hubbard Series: Humanitarian—Education, Literacy & Civilization*). Of particular interest here, however, is Ron's progress through that New York Institute of Photography course as the

parallel field of study wherein he first examined crucial barriers to learning.

Correspondence tells all: "I have a lesson query," begins an LRH letter to Institute instructors, and specifically cites difficulties with certain misused or misdefined words. The greater point: If the misunderstood or undefined word is now broadly acknowledged as the primary stumbling block to all general education, and inabilities to *apply* what one learns, then herein lies the LRH trail to defining that barrier.

Below
Long view of Saint Hill Manor (in background left of center), 1964

Left Saint Hill Manor, East Grinstead, England, 1964

Overlooking East Grinstead, England, with his Jaguar XK 150 "camera car"

Above With Micro-Press, Brighton, England, 1965

Below The Micro-Press

Here, too, lies the fully personal perspective on the matter, as in: "I don't want a piece of this course all clouded up. I want it all where I can use it. In my head." Consequently, while an LRH secretary tells of scouring local libraries for photographic dictionaries, that LRH letter to Institute instructors requested a clarification of terms relating to "Special Printing Processes." Similarly, while every student utilizing L. Ron Hubbard Study Technology appreciates problems of "too steep a study gradient," or the fact one cannot master a skill without having grasped the necessary previous step, here

is Ron unraveling the matter with key questions on the sequence of photograph retouching lessons.

There is more: Here is also Ron coming to terms with technical advancements in the field and so embarking upon the second phase of a sixty-year career. As a first broad word on that next phase to follow, he now speaks of a forte in terms of not only *action* and *candid,* but *color.* As a word of explanation, one must bear in mind that color film was most temperamental through these years. Indeed, if the color snapshot is now common currency across the

realms of popular photography, with billions of reasonably true snapshots rolling off commercial processors, the world was not always so colorful. Professional color film of the early 1960s required extraordinary care as regards exposure and processing, and many an old-line professional never even bothered crossing that imposing line from black and white. In contrast—and more will be said on the matter through pages to follow—the lengths to which Ron went for the perfectly rendered color photograph were equally extraordinary. In addition to exhaustive testing of films, processing and printing techniques,

Above
Railroad switching station, East Grinstead, England, 1964

Above
Beech grove,
southern
England, 1965

Right
Outside East
Grinstead,
England, 1964

these were further years of extensive and, actually, quite rarefied testing of tinted filters to control the rendering of colors. Also quite rarefied was his testing of flash and studio lighting; hence, the note from a London dealer:

> *"Dear Mr. Hubbard,*
> *"Your experience with flash equipment is of moment, since we have not yet carried out extensive tests under such conditions, and we are requested to supply information of a general nature, and your experiments have added to the store of knowledge concerning the characteristics of [our] film."*

And still there was more: By way of introduction to his greater philosophic examination of aesthetics as a whole, published today as *ART,* Ron particularly cites Saint Hill photographic studies as materially assisting in a final codification of all artistic endeavor. While for a sense of those studies and the depth of his examination, we come to an LRH exchange with a British Colour Council on his search for some means of actually measuring human emotional response to any given hue. Most especially, he wished to know if the Council had developed a dependable system with which to compute the emotional effect of color. That the Council had not would eventually lead to Ron's further examination of general marketing theories on color associations, also discussed through the pages of *ART.* Yet for the moment, he could at least rest assured, "I know where we are now in this area of science and art and so can go on happily without being haunted by the possible existence of a flawless system."

As for a sense of how he went on happily through the latter days of 1964, we hear of an

New Photographic Vistas from Saint Hill   85

LRH chauffeur regularly appearing in the Manor courtyard at two o'clock in the afternoon to load cameras, tripods and assorted gear into the boot of Ron's utterly classic Jaguar or a formidably large (at least along narrow English country roads) Pontiac Bonneville. Typically, shots were fully preconceived—meadows, lanes and parklands previously scouted for ideal vantage points, general composition firmly in mind. Then again, shoots from these days were frequently scripted—as in ninety-seven sequenced shots for the Scientology brochure "A Student Comes to Saint Hill" or a forty-two-frame photographic essay of neighboring East Grinstead and eventually comprising the definitive East Grinstead visitor's guide. The latter, incidentally, further required specialized skills of photographic copy work to successfully incorporate original George Cruikshank illustrations for a somewhat Dickensian air; while all residents featured in the shoot (very much including the railway switchman pictured on page 83) were finally presented with framed prints of their portraits.

Thereafter, LRH cameras were regularly seen along Sussex lanes on behalf of either local shops and attractions or Scientology organizations. As a summary word, Ron would soon describe these days in terms of applying photography intensively to the benefit of immediate concerns; while to underscore the statement he tallied several thousand color frames through but four months of those Saint Hill afternoons. By the same token, however, and this as long-standing policy: *"I won't take a photograph of anybody or photographs for anybody unless I feel it will do them some good."*

Left
Nursery dahlias, southern England, 1965

Above With Rollei, at terrace steps, Saint Hill Manor, England, 1964

The Rolleiflex Collection

A favorite of professionals through the 1940s, the twin-lens Rolleiflex still remains a legendary camera. To be sure, no less than sheer engineering quality finally priced the twin-lens out of the market. The working principle was simple enough. The photographer views the image through the "view" lens, while a second "taking" lens records the image on film. Because the two lenses are precisely coupled by precision gears, when the view lens is focused, the taking lens likewise turns to focus. Consequently, what one sees through the focusing lens is exactly the focus of the primary lens exposing the film. Hence, the necessity of real engineering quality to ensure perfect synchronization of movement between the two lenses, i.e., that when one focused the view lens, the taking lens indeed came into perfect focus. Because the twin-lens viewing system does not rely upon the movable mirrors found within single-lens reflex cameras,

mechanics of operation were particularly vibration free and so eliminated blurring problems from the vibration of moving mirrors. The camera was available in several models, each permanently fitted with a specific pair of lenses. In other words, and unlike modern cameras with interchangeable lenses, if one wished to switch from a wide-angle lens to a telephoto lens, one had to have another entire *camera* fitted with a telephoto lens. Thus the need for an extensive collection of Rolleis for any serious Rollei photographer. Nonetheless, the name is still remembered for a rare versatility—simultaneously serving Jacques-Yves Cousteau three hundred feet beneath the sea and Sir John Hunt along the face of Mount Everest. For just that versatility, then, one finds Ron with a Rollei from mild English pastureland to a blistering African veldt. Also included was a complementary flash attachment to bat off those shots "faster than scat." ■

The Saint Hill Darkroom

"THIS IS AN ENTIRELY UTILITARIAN darkroom," read a note of explanation, and LRH catalogued features in terms of two sinks, five beehive safelights, numerous electrical outlets, storage cabinets, outside dryer and a flatbed glazer for a finishing gloss on prints. His point: here was "a very easy darkroom to use." Not so easy was the final selection of equipment and honing of procedures for a fully *standard* developing and printing line.

The matter is critical—and especially so in an age before digital photography, when variables of processing and printing posed real problems for those in search of consistently standard results. To cite but one example: when developing color film, even a single degree of variation in chemical temperatures can negatively affect the outcome. Detail in shadows, brightness of highlights, general clarity and contrast, not to mention accurate reproduction

of colors—all significantly determined by what takes place in darkroom developing baths. Indeed, without a truly standard developing line, one could easily process the same shot on three different occasions only to print three radically different photographs—and not a one resembling the shot originally envisioned through the viewfinder.

Ron's Saint Hill darkroom, then, represented precisely that dependable standard to a predictable result: every step and process codified and documented, every piece of equipment fully tested in. Similarly, and just as methodically, he tested in every type of film: how *that* particular film best handled shadows and responded to highlights, what range of light and shadow it recorded and, of course, the best means of processing—all carefully predetermined before exposing even a single frame on location. The net result: the elimination of all variables and a technical mastery across the whole of his Saint Hill photographic line. Or even more simply: the shot Ron first envisioned in a viewfinder was, indeed, the photograph he finally presented.

Needless to say, establishing that standard required a lot: "I need your advices on what you now consider your proper manufactures and procedures," read a 1964 request to a regional distributor. Whereupon he followed with three typewritten pages on darkroom equipment and chemicals in the name of "brilliant, wonderfully clear negatives and prints." Similarly aimed letters tell of an equally extensive search for enlargers and lights, and all while simultaneously training a first darkroom assistant/apprentice. Finally, and bearing in mind just how critical is every individual factor in the production of quality photographs: "Every few years I am faced with sufficient changes in films, papers and chemicals to have to groove in an entirely new photographic regimen."

The Rear Screen Projector

DATING FROM THE SUMMER OF 1964 IS an especially telling LRH letter to Ascot Lamps & Lighting Ltd. of London. Specifically under discussion was Ron's construction and honing of his Saint Hill rear screen projection system. By way of brief explanation, that system was described in terms of a "picture projected from behind background screen as in fashion photography—girl appears to be in Venice, etc."

Not remarked upon, but relevant to any discussion of Ron's employment of screen projection, was his long and creative research trail. In point of fact, his Saint Hill screen projection system was a linear descendant of a 1947 LRH invention dubbed the "Photo-Scenic Projector," and particularly suited for a small studio or a theatrical stage. Also not remarked upon were the truly challenging difficulties in both constructing a first Saint Hill screen projection system and honing its use.

The problem is actually twofold. While simple enough in design—black and white or colored slides are projected onto a screen for an "anywhere" backdrop—the system requires exceptionally precise alignment of subject, camera, projector and screen. If less

than precise, the subject's shadow appears in the photograph as a most unnatural halo. In the second place, one must just as perfectly arrange the lighting to ensure the subject actually appears located in the background scene—seated in the same afternoon sunlight, for example, as originally captured in the projected image. Both sides of the problem become all the more troublesome when—as presented here—that screen is employed for self-portraiture. (After all, the self-portrait requires the photographer *in front* of the camera and so he cannot possibly look through the lens—the *only* perspective from which one

Above
Ron's photographic studio in Saint Hill Manor, with rear projection screen and Deardorff camera

Below
Rear screen projected background for self-portrait, with Voigtländer, Saint Hill Manor, 1965

Left Self-portrait, with Linhof and using rear screen projected background, Saint Hill Manor, 1965

Above
Self-portrait,
with Voigtländer
and rear screen
projected
background,
Saint Hill Manor,
1965

Far right
Self-portrait,
with Linhof
Technika, rear
screen projected
background,
Saint Hill Manor,
1965

can assess if all is correctly aligned for shots against a projected screen image.) Hence, the continual LRH references to many minute adjustments of lighting and equipment.

Then again, an LRH assistant still speaks of searching high and low for the actual screen with which Ron first fashioned his then quite novel system.

Rear Screen Projection System

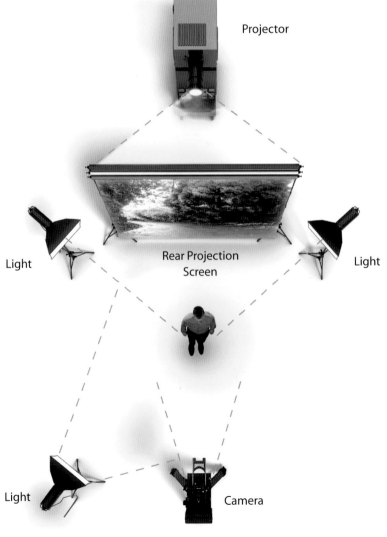

Projector

Light

Rear Projection
Screen

Light

Light

Camera

Letter to Professor Land

ALTHOUGH POPULARLY ASSOCIATED with amateur use, the Polaroid Land Camera has also long served the professional. In particular, the "Polaroid back," fitted to a larger-format camera, provided a near-instantaneous test print of lighting and composition. Immediately intrigued with the Polaroid potential, Ron was soon engaged in testing the camera. What in turn followed—in the interests of Polaroid, better snapshots and happier photographers—came Ron's letter to Professor Land.

Above
With Polaroid
Land Automatic
100, Saint Hill,
England, 1964

Left LRH's Polaroid Land Automatic 100

Professor Land,
Polaroid Corporation,
730 Main Street,
CAMBRIDGE, Massachusetts 02139,
U.S.A.

Dear Professor Land:

Re: SOME MARKETING SUGGESTIONS

Some years ago (1956) I wrote you that blue flash made better B & W pictures than white. Your engineering department courteously replied and, while I suppose the blue flash now used is only because of color film, and is probably not an outgrowth of my suggestion, I note that it *is* used which pleases me.

After having several Land cameras and backs, I just received a 100 and at once got to work with it. What a splendid creation! My congratulations. Your genius is fully attested.

There are one or two small things I'd like to comment on in your presentation of this camera. As a professional in the field of research and development you might find my bits of some use.

SHUTTER SPEED:

I have tested out the 100 and find that you have not made a point adequately to your customers which could be very damaging to your sales.

You are possibly following Eastman's early promotional pattern in many ways. The first Eastman marketing ideas were very sound. "Snapshot" "Box Camera" "Anybody can take a picture" "Few gimmicks to know" etc. are all fine....

You've inherited a bad bug in shutter speed.... Actually it blurs pictures when hand held. The amount of blur is too small for the amateur to recognize it as blur. They just blame the camera.

Blur isn't acceptable to amateurs. They see pro quality only in sharpness. Blur = amateur. Sharp = pro. That's their index.

Your new 100 and the 3000 film are capable of fantastic sharpness.

But this new 100 shutter speed won't give it to the amateur.

Even the 1/50th speed of a flash bulb isn't fast enough to prevent hand-held cameras from blurring in most hands.

I put this 100 on a tripod where it belongs and I'm getting sharp pictures with flash and available that makes the amateur user blink.

For instance, my mother was an amateur photographer. But she gave it up because she never could get a sharp picture. Then I gave her a Rolleicord and nailed its shutter at a 1/250th…and she got right back into it, burning film by the hundreds of yards. Her pictures were wonderful and SHARP.

If amateurs cannot get sharp, well-exposed pictures they don't burn film. They don't even take pictures.

Every time an amateur has a bad series of failures he burns less film. It's harder to get going again. Give him several such loses and he lays the camera away.…

Continual failures to get a decently exposed, sharp picture means an amateur slowing up on picture taking or stopping altogether.

You have set up 100 users, I am afraid, for a lot of failures on blur.

This color film and shutter speed don't give sharp color pictures when hand held.

I don't think this 100 *can* be hand held for optimum results even with flash. I can hold down to 1/30th but in British dull light, the 100 gets blur. I know you're supposed to wait for the second click but you *still* get enough blur to spoil pro quality.

This is harsh judgment but given in good spirit. You don't have to rebuild any cameras.

All you have to do is tell these people in their instruction manual that if they want super-sharp pictures to use a cable release or self-timer and a *tripod*. Tripods didn't stop the amateur in 1920, why should they in 1964?

The self-timer is a misnomer. It's a Blurless Shutter Release. I shoot all scenics with a "self-timer" on a small tripod and the results are lovely. A self-timer ought to be capable of firing in 2 seconds, only time for tripod vibration to die.

My conclusion, for using the 100, subject to my becoming the Rock of Gibraltar, is that on B & W and color on the 100 I *must* use a tripod and shoot with a self-timer or cable release. And I'm making an older 100 user here gasp at what can be done that way.

It's a lovely camera and I'm making it work. But that box camera potential shutter speed is costing people pictures—and you sales and above all, film sales. You are losing your camera buyers as picture-takers more often than you suppose. It's *very* easy to lose an amateur picture-taker. All you have to do is give him a few bad pictures. And he quits.…

INSTRUCTION BOOK:

People *will* study from simple texts. I'm surprised you don't issue a small number of instruction books anyway as a promotional idea. Five small pamphlets on how to take various things each under a different type of picture. The Land is so far removed from older photography that old style photography instruction books don't apply. Thus a Land Camera operator tends to stultify. He's got nothing to graduate to, no method of advance. No texts to study....

As it is you sell a camera and forget the user and you lose out on film sales.

You *could* move Land operators up to advanced amateur easily if you taught them how. They don't know and there's no way for them to learn as old photo manuals, they think—and rightly—don't apply.

They receive 5 books, study each and answer the exam in the back of the book, mail it in. You mark it and send it back. When you've got 5 answer sheets and the pictures you require, you send them a Land Photographer certificate and everybody's happy....

Your promotion is a bit on the inhuman side, understandable due to your wonderful technical achievements. But PEOPLE use them.

The Land Camera will go as far as the public takes it.

Of course I'd see it that way since I'm the expert on people. But biased or not there's truth in this view.

If you cut off technically from the old, you have to assume the full burden of pushing the new.

And a needed part of any newness is thorough education.

You're a revolution in photography. But a revolution without complete re-education potential can fail....

All this is sent in a very helpful frame of mind.

The 100 is pure genius....

No claim, fees, or recompense of any kind attaches to any of my suggestions. You have probably thought of most of this, so regard my suggestions as a viewpoint from a user, not a criticism of your excellent product.

Sincerely,

L. Ron Hubbard

Top Polaroid of Saint Hill grounds, England, 1964

Bottom Polaroid of Weir Wood Reservoir, East Grinstead, England, 1964

Sir Robert Fossett's Circus

Above
With Rollei at Sir Robert Fossett's Circus, 1964

Right
Entrance to the big top, 1964

"*As you might have heard,*" Ron remarked through the course of a later lecture, "*and which you saw the evidence of, I went to a circus on the invitation of its management and photographed the various acts.*" The circus in question was Sir Robert Fossett's animal menagerie and big-top extravaganza, replete with lion tamers, elephant trainers, acrobats and clowns. The shoot took place over three evenings in June of 1964, ultimately consumed nearly four hundred color slides and posed a considerable challenge of variable lighting under the

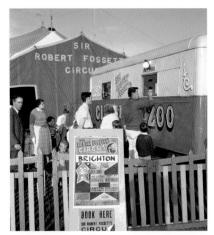

big top. Also challenging were uncomfortably close encounters with rolling elephants and cracking whips, as in: "The Elephant Man, there, he's got quite a sense of humor. He keeps putting an elephant over on top of me every time I start shooting his act. Elephant will sweep in right dead-close to where I'm sitting. The other night, why, he popped a whip in front of my face—not more than an inch or two away from my cheek. Of course, they're experts at

this sort of thing. See if I'd blink. And I just grinned at him."

Then again, to capture a leaping lion, Ron tells of carefully timing the shot, not to the animal's movement, but a trainer's one-finger signal to the big, poised cat. "So the second I saw the finger go up I clicked the shutter." Although so intense was the concentration, only after clicking the shutter did he realize he had actually pressed himself shoulder-to-flank with the lion's mate. Also of note was Ron's slide show presentation to circus crew and performers—likewise under the big top and with images projected onto a twelve-by-twelve feet square hand-sewn sheet. Finally—and remembering that LRH dictum "I won't take a photograph of anybody or photographs for anybody unless I feel it will do them some good"—we come to what originally sparked that Sir Robert Fossett invitation to shoot.

Upon first reaching the circus encampment, Ron actually found the big top only scantily filled.

Top
Sir Robert Fossett Circus' mobile "box office"

Bottom
The performing seals. One of nearly four hundred frames from Ron's Rollei.

Top
The "Elephant Man," 1964

Bottom left
Timing this shot to the trainer's finger signal, Ron captured the big cat midleap, 1964

Bottom right
Ron's "The Comedy Horse" from his three-day photo shoot of Sir Robert Fossett's Circus, 1964

In a slightly later note to circus management and crew, Ron would summarize the problem as "The public is not attending public events such as circuses in the numbers heretofore experienced." Contributing factors were complex, and included both inadequate word of mouth and the advent of televised circus acts. But in either case, Sir Robert had requested help. In reply, Ron would finally present a thirty-page dissection of the "Good show–No attendance" problem and precisely how that problem might be resolved with low-cost advertising and virtually cost-free promotion. Yet more immediately came the local

publication of some thirty LRH photographs from the big top. What next ensued was rightly described as a veritable torrent of community support and publicity. Indeed, when a local town council revoked Sir Robert's rental of circus grounds, no less than a mayor and chief of police turned out to help with the relocation... At which point those tents were soon erected atop a highly visible knoll and, coupled with a timely appearance of newspaper articles, one could no longer even hear that clicking camera amidst gasps and cheers to the rafters.

Above
Seals returning to their trailer for a well-deserved break

Selections for Exhibition

"*Please send me entry forms for your Photographic Salon Exhibitions.*" The subsequent LRH submission included a selection of Sussex landscapes and pastorals, an English river scenic and his East Grinstead "Study in Three Dimensions." Although quite confident of photographs in themselves, Ron was plainly under no illusion as to

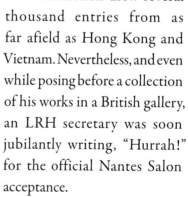

competition. In point of fact, that 9th Nantes International Salon Exhibition drew several thousand entries from as far afield as Hong Kong and Vietnam. Nevertheless, and even while posing before a collection of his works in a British gallery, an LRH secretary was soon jubilantly writing, "Hurrah!" for the official Nantes Salon acceptance.

Above
The award-winning "Autumn Sky," southern England, 1964

Left
At London photo exhibit, 1965

Top
Southern English
countryside,
1965

Bottom
Equestrian,
East Grinstead,
England, 1965

Far left
Cedar of
Lebanon, Saint
Hill, England,
1965

A fox hunt in Sussex, shot with a cherished Rolleiflex, 1964

Above Sussex pastureland through the lens of a Deardorff, 1964

The Deardorff

While tending to evoke quaint images of nineteenth-century photographers, the Deardorff continues to enjoy professional renown for studio work, architecture and grand-scale landscapes. The camera is handmade—originally in salvaged mahogany from Prohibition-era bar tops out of Chicago—and folds up in remarkable ways: "like a Japanese puzzle box," or so Ron remarked. The LRH Deardorff dates from early September 1964, and was acquired from a London Camera Exchange where dealers soon received Ron's note of gratitude for "initiating us into the intricacies of the Deardorff." Forty-eight hours later, upon returning from a Sussex field shoot, he was already describing that camera as an "old reliable." ■

Self-Portraits

AMONG THE MOST REPRINTED SHOTS from the whole of the L. Ron Hubbard photographic archives, Ron's mid-1960s self-portraits represent a culmination of extensive film and lighting tests. His primary cameras were the Linhof and Deardorff—classic studio view cameras, with large film *sheets* to record images with a far greater wealth of detail than smaller-format films. For still greater detail, Ron further employed glass-backed negatives.

To explain: While film emulsion is typically affixed to a flexible celluloid base, emulsion on a glass-backed negative is inflexible and does not bend. The glass-backed negative, then, remains perfectly aligned to the lens, and even if imperceptible on a snapshot, when discussing large-format negatives, that perfect alignment yields dramatically increased detail. To be sure, when discussing the glass-backed negative, one is actually discussing the ultimate in image clarity.

Also employed in self-portraits was the Rolleiflex, rigged with an exceptionally long pneumatic cable release, i.e., a rubber tube attached to the camera's shutter release mechanism (squeezing an air bulb forces air down the tube and so trips the shutter).

Self-portraits from Rhodesia, 1966

Far left
To take this self-portrait, Ron used his Rollei and a mirror, 1965

Using
glass-backed
negatives
(which remain
perfectly aligned
to the lens
and thus yield
dramatically
increased detail
and clarity),
Ron shot these
self-portraits at
Saint Hill in 1959

For Ron's full-length pose in his Saint Hill garden, that tube was carefully concealed beneath a trouser leg. Yet eventually noting even slightly tensing muscles from squeezing the bulb tended to effect an expression, he would further experiment with an infrared shutter release triggered by the mere movement of a finger. Yet cameras and techniques aside, here are the photographs most requested by Scientologists and Scientology organizations...which is to say, here is LRH. ■

Above With Linhof view camera,
Saint Hill grounds, 1965

The Linhof

A beauty of a view camera, or so Ron described the Linhof 5 × 7 in continual use through his latter Saint Hill years. As noted, the Linhof was one of three cameras employed for self-portraits, and also particularly suited for fieldwork. Then again, many a reader may have rightly wondered how Ron managed his broadly reprinted still life of five Chinese miniatures, alternately in and out of focus. In fact, he photographed only one, exposing five views of the same miniature on the same Linhof film plate. The technique is known as multiple exposure and, in this case, Ron accomplished the shot with repeated steps of shooting the miniature in focus, then repositioning the miniature and shooting out of focus, repositioning and shooting in focus, etc. ∎

Left Ron's 5 × 7 (left) and 4 × 5 (right)
Linhof field view cameras

The Linhof   121

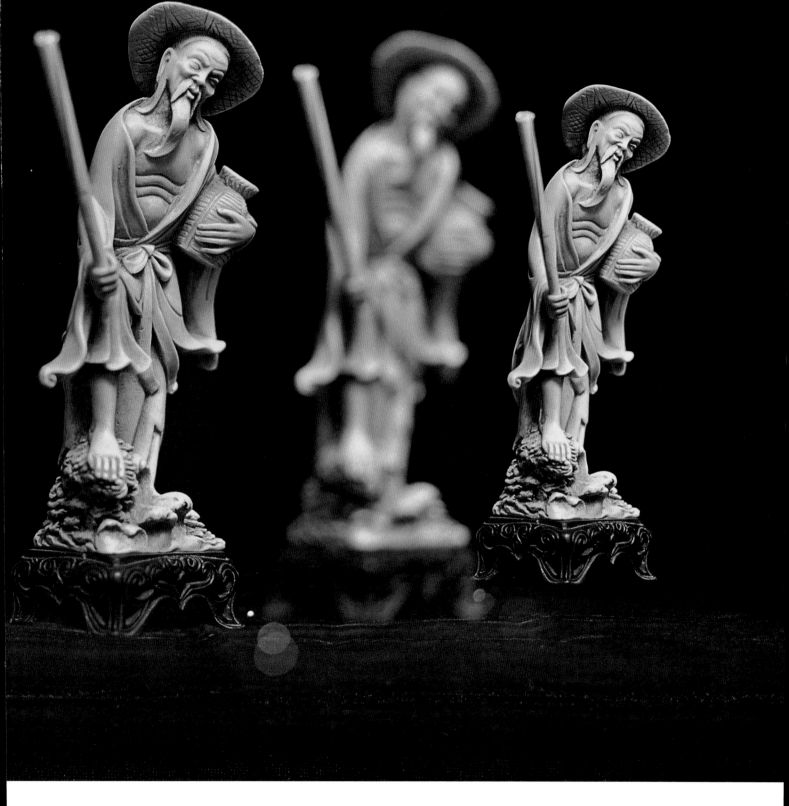

Multiple exposure of Chinese figure using the Linhof

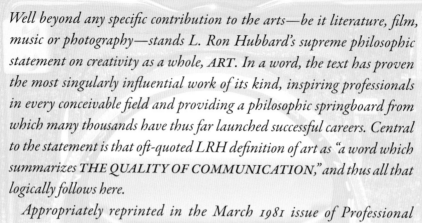

Well beyond any specific contribution to the arts—be it literature, film, music or photography—stands L. Ron Hubbard's supreme philosophic statement on creativity as a whole, *ART*. In a word, the text has proven the most singularly influential work of its kind, inspiring professionals in every conceivable field and providing a philosophic springboard from which many thousands have thus far launched successful careers. Central to the statement is that oft-quoted LRH definition of art as "a word which summarizes THE QUALITY OF COMMUNICATION," and thus all that logically follows here.

Appropriately reprinted in the March 1981 issue of *Professional Photographer*, and yet again in a 1997 issue of Britain's *Darkroom User*, the essay was presented in reply to that long-debated question on the photograph as art or craft. That is, does the "pure" photograph, as Ansel Adams and others of his circle proclaimed, constitute a work of art in its own right? Or is it merely a scientifically crafted reflection of nature's artistry?

IS IT ART?

by L. RON HUBBARD

WHEN A WORK OF painting, music or other form attains two-way communication, it is truly art.

One occasionally hears an artist being criticized on the basis that his work is too "literal" or too "common." But one has rarely if ever heard any definition of "literal" or "common." And there are many artists simply hung up on this, protesting it. Also, some avant-garde schools go completely over the cliff in avoiding anything "literal" or "common"—and indeed go completely out of communication!

The *return* flow from the person viewing a work would be contribution. True art always elicits a contribution from those who view or hear or experience it. By *contribution* is meant "adding to it."

An illustration is "literal" in that it tells everything there is to know. Let us say the illustration is a picture of a tiger approaching a chained girl. It does not really matter how well the painting is executed, it remains an illustration and it IS literal. But now let us take a small portion out of the scene and enlarge it. Let us take, say, the head of the tiger with its baleful eye and snarl. Suddenly we no longer have an illustration. It is no longer "literal." And the reason lies in the fact that the viewer can fit this expression into his own concepts, ideas or experience: he can supply the why of the snarl, he can compare the head to someone he knows. In short, he can CONTRIBUTE to the head.

The skill with which the head is executed determines the degree of response.

Because the viewer can contribute to the picture, it is art.

In music, the hearer can contribute his own emotion or motion. And even if the music is only a single drum, if it elicits a contribution of emotion or motion, it is truly art.

That work which delivers everything and gets little or nothing in return is not art. The "common" or overused melody, the expected shape or form gets little or no contribution from the hearer or viewer. That work which is too unclear or too poorly executed may get no contribution.

Incidental to this, one can ask if a photograph can ever be art, a controversy which has been raging for a century or more. One could say that it is only difficult to decide because one has to establish how much the photographer has contributed to the "reality" or "literalness" in front of his camera, how he has interpreted it, but really the point is whether or not that photograph elicits a contribution from its viewer. If it does, it is art.

"When a work of painting, music or other form attains two-way communication, it is truly art."

Innovation plays a large role in all works which may become art. But even this can be overdone. Originality can be overdone to the point where it is no longer within any possible understanding by those viewing or hearing it. One can be so original one goes entirely outside the most distant perimeter of agreement with his viewers or listeners. Sometimes this is done, one suspects, when one has not spent the labor necessary to execute the work. Various excuses are assigned such an action, the most faulty of which is "self-satisfaction" of the artist. While it is quite all right to commune with oneself, one cannot also then claim that it is art if it communicates with no one else and no other's communication is possible.

The third flow, of people talking to one another about a work, can also be considered a communication and, where it occurs, is a valid contribution as it makes the work known.

Destructive attitudes about a work can be considered as a refusal to contribute. Works that are shocking or bizarre to a point of eliciting protest may bring to themselves notoriety thereby and may shake things up, but when the refusal to contribute is too widespread, such works tend to disqualify as art.

There is also the matter of divided opinion about a work. Some contribute to it, some refuse to contribute to it. In such cases one must examine who is contributing and who is refusing. One can then say that it is a work of art to those who contribute to it and that it is not to those who refuse to contribute to it.

Criticism is some sort of index of degree of contribution. There are, roughly, two types of criticism: one can be called "invalidative criticism," the other "constructive criticism."

Invalidative criticism is all too prevalent in the arts, for there exist such things as "individual taste," contemporary standards and, unfortunately, even envy or jealousy. Too often, criticism is simply an individual refusal to contribute. One could also state that "Those who destructively criticize can't do."

"Constructive criticism" is a term which is often used but seldom defined. But it has use. It could probably be best defined as criticism which "indicates a better way to do," at least in the opinion of the critic. Those who simply find fault and never suggest a practical means of doing it better rather forfeit their right to criticize.

Art is probably the most uncodified and least organized of all fields. It therefore acquires to itself the most "authorities." Usually nothing is required of an "authority" except to say what is right, wrong, good, bad, acceptable or unacceptable. Too often the sole qualification of the "authority" (as in poor teaching of some subjects) is a memorized list of objects and their creators and dates with some hazy idea of what the work was. An "authority" could considerably improve his status by using rather precise definitions of his terms. The modern trend of seeking the significance in what the artist meant is of course not likely to advance the arts very much.

Viewing and experiencing art on the basis of what one is contributing to it and what others contribute to it is a workable approach. And it would result in improved art and improved appreciation.

Such a viewpoint, interestingly, also includes some things into the field of art not previously so viewed.

Las Palmas Harbor, Grand Canary, 1965

CHAPTER FIVE

A Photographic
HOLIDAY

A Photographic
Holiday

WHAT RON DESCRIBED AS HIS SPANISH PHOTOGRAPHIC Holiday commenced in the first week of January 1965. In fact, however, the shoot was not strictly pleasure, and the bulk of photographs, including Canary Island historical sites and an especially rustic bullfight, were actually commissioned by a national tourist office. Still, he retained wide latitude in selecting subjects, while several pages of tape-recorded notes provide us with a rare sense of how he worked.

For example, to candidly capture joys of Canary Island tariff-free shops, Ron speaks of enlisting an assistant to engage a local merchant in lively bargaining for a pair of binoculars before discreetly shooting from an adjacent market stall. Similarly, he speaks of stepping to a hotel window, catching sight of anchored white ships and terra-cotta colored masts, and hurriedly descending through rubble-strewn lanes to a Las Palmas sea wall. Then, what with patchy light under shifting clouds, "It took quite a while to disentangle the sun and shadow." Likewise Ron's shoot of a looming Maspalomas lighthouse required a fair degree of diligence, beginning with a cross-island drive along rain-swept roads in a rattletrap red Austin. ("It won't go into reverse unless you put about 60 pounds of pressure sideways on its gearshift and it is, in fact, rather a highly unsatisfactory car.")

Below
Lighthouse at Maspalomas, Grand Canary Island, 1965

Left With Graphex, Grand Canary Island, 1965

Above "Looked over the countryside—rather striking
volcanic countryside"—LRH, Grand Canary Island, 1965

Upon reaching a Maspalomas shoreline, he further found what the local picture postcards suggested: if frequently photographed in the name of tourist appeal, that remote lighthouse was not especially photogenic. Moreover, to gain a classically composed perspective required an exceedingly long tramp across seemingly limitless sands.

There is more, including difficulties in turning "ghastly gray" skies to a vibrant blue with locally purchased filters and angling in for interesting views of otherwise monotonous

Above Overlooking Gibraltar, 1965

Nikonos Underwater Camera

Although obviously intended for the deep-sea photographer, the Nikonos underwater camera admirably served Ron through all wet and heavy weather. The case in point were his shots from a mist-drenched cliff at Gibraltar, where salt air and moisture might well have played havoc with the Rollei or Graflex. Moreover, the Nikonos is both reasonably light and compact, and so served as a most convenient backup camera for Grand Canary shoots of sand-blown dunes and smoky nightclubs. ∎

palms. In summary, however, and perhaps shedding a little light on why that Spanish tourist bureau had so eagerly engaged him: while the island may have offered some truly promising pictures, "you have to work for them hard."

Above With Voigtländer at local riding academy, East Grinstead, England, 1965

The Voigtländer

The first to provide a built-in flash and first 35mm to offer a zoom lens, the Voigtländer was nothing if not innovative. Hence, Ron's unqualified praise of the camera; he actually described the Voigtländer Ultramatic as the singularly best all-around 35mm of the day. In consequence, a Voigtländer long stood at the ready on a corner of his desk, and served him through many a shoot beyond the Canaries.

Additionally part of Ron's Voigtländer system is a long-focus 200mm lens initially employed from the bleachers of the *Plaza de Toros*. As a matter of fact, Ron actually purchased the lens barely three hours before a first bull entered the ring. ■

Right Ron's Voigtländer camera system, which he described as the singular best all-around 35mm of its day

Flamenco Dancers

"HAD A BEAUTIFUL DINNER AND watched some flamenco dancers who were very loud with their heels," Ron recorded on an otherwise peaceful January 5th evening in his Las Palmas hotel room. Yet, given no portfolio for a Grand Canary tourist board was complete without those quick-heeled dancers, he returned to the club on the following evening with Rollei, Nikonos and Graflex. Then followed a deft maneuvering through hand-clapping revelers to a forefront table and a calculated attracting of the dancer's eye with his Mecablitz flash.... Until, as he so pointedly phrased it, "They danced to me, and I got the pictures."

The Bullfight

"THE WHOLE SUBJECT OF BULLFIGHTING," Ron confessed, "is something that surfeits one very easily." Nevertheless, and with blessings from that Spanish tourist bureau, he proceeded by taxi to a *Plaza de Toros* on January 17, with Rollei, Graflex and a Voigtländer Bessamatic now fitted with a newly purchased 200mm lens for close views from far away.

Succeeding notes are hardly less explicit than the photographs. Although authorized to shoot from a barricaded press box on the bullring floor, he finally chose the higher and less obstructed view from shaded bleachers (although not without the occasional obstruction from excitedly jostling fans). As a general word on action shooting from afar, he spoke of "constant tracking," i.e., "you always have to have your camera in focus on the principal things you are going to shoot." Otherwise, "It's there and it's gone." (Automatic focusing cameras, developed to facilitate precisely this problem with action shots, were not to appear for almost twenty years.) As regards the spectacle at hand, he noted provincial bullfights were infamously bloody, with brave but inexperienced matadors and equally brave but young bulls. ("The old bulls are the real tough ones.") Moreover, "this is about as far as you can get from the standpoint of professional bullfighting."

What then ensued amply proved the point. First to appear was a "butcher to end all butchers," who could not drive a blade home "with the bull dead, motionless and hypnotized." Next came an equally fervid stabber, known as *El Tercer Hombre,* who nearly took a horn through the head, followed by yet another who stabbed in excess before finally limping off with a badly gashed leg. Needless to say, Ron dryly concluded, "None of this went off calmly," but he still managed eighty-five color photographs of that "bloody-minded" business in a far-flung provincial bullring. ■

Funchal, island of Madeira

CHAPTER SIX

PORTS OF CALL

Ports of Call

WHILE L. RON HUBBARD'S 1967 MOVE FROM SAINT HILL Manor to a 3,200-ton research vessel, *Apollo,* is rightfully regarded as a wholly new chapter in the greater story of Scientology expansion, one might also see that move in terms of wholly new photographic vistas. Beginnings were modest. Glancing from a research room porthole at two o'clock in the afternoon, one hears of Ron catching sight of a Lisbon docked tanker and immediately calling for his Pentax. Similarly, between long bouts of research, he would call for the loading of saddlebags on a blue Triumph motorcycle (or a later Harley-Davidson) with cameras—typically the Voigtländer Ultramatic or Voigtländer Bessamatic. Then again, when Ron typically called for a camera on deck, aides soon noted, "We bring out the Koni Rapid Omega." Also noted, a research room desk drawer was to regularly contain: one bottle of liquid adhesive for cementing slide mounts, two magnifying glasses for viewing negatives, cotton gloves and scissors for cutting strips of negatives and six empty canisters awaiting spent rolls of film. But the salient point is finally and only this: directly beside freshly drafted LRH Technical Bulletins and LRH Policy Letters for the greater advancement of Scientology, one *always* found an LRH camera.

In the main, that camera was employed for two ends: documentary or promotional shots on behalf of Scientology, and the same again for local industries and tourist boards. As for a few incidental notes: Island landscapes and harbor seascapes intended for tourist brochures were frequently subjects of shoots from Ron's motorcycle excursions. Before photographing a famed Tower of Belém at the mouth of a Lisbon estuary, he spent a quiet hour considering not merely photographic perspectives but the greater historical perspective of a famed local monument originally erected to clock departures and arrivals of Portuguese mariners. When shooting a Moroccan port of Agadir from the window of his research room, he was

On the flying bridge of his research yacht, *Apollo,* 1972

Above With Rollei 35, aboard his Chris Craft,
North Africa, 1968

The Rollei 35

The extremely compact Rollei 35, virtually fitting in
the palm of one's hand, was frequently used by LRH
on photo excursions from the *Apollo* to North Africa,
Spain and Portugal. ∎

yet again testing film and filters for optimum color rendition. Hence, the entry in an LRH photographic log relating to the fact that the film was not reacting optimally due to the color of light in his geographic location: "That the blue tinge I thought was bad film is actually shooting color in light that is too blue." But in either case—and this to a student of the day—if photography is, indeed, light writing, then *"you can make light do anything you want."* ▪

Above
"Cathedral lighting effect" off Las Palmas, Grand Canary Island, 1967

Left
Sunset from the deck of the *Apollo,* at Agadir, Morocco, 1970

"Before photographing a famed Tower of Belém at the mouth of a Lisbon estuary, he spent a quiet hour considering not merely photographic perspectives but the greater historical perspective..."

Tower of Belém, adjacent to Lisbon harbor, 1973

Above Self-portrait from the Gandolfi,
aboard the *Apollo*, 1972

The Gandolfi

"I was very delighted and surprised to receive this wonderful Gandolfi 5 × 4 view portrait camera for my birthday. It was still ice cold from being 75,000 feet up.

"In return we'll whip out some new photos for orgs and releases.

"Thank all of you so very much for this gift."
—LRH, 26 March 1970

Additionally remarked upon in Ron's letter of appreciation to Scientology staff: the lens was ideally suited for portraits, and all accessories were otherwise perfect for portraiture needs of the moment.

Not, of course, remarked upon was the later history of LRH self-portraits from his wonderful Gandolfi. That is, from that very camera came the singularly most viewed self-portrait in the whole of the LRH collection: the dust-jacket photograph for Ron's multimillion-selling novels, *Battlefield Earth* and the ten-volume *Mission Earth* dekalogy. ■

Left The Gandolfi 5 × 4 view portrait camera—a 1970 birthday present from Scientology staff

Above With Mamiya C33, *Apollo,* 1972

Mamiya C33

"We are interested in Japanese cameras because of the very superior lenses," reads an LRH query from 1964 to the Japan Camera Industry Association. Of particular interest was the medium-format, twin-lens Mamiya C33, providing suitably sized negatives for magazine reproduction. Among the first medium-format "systems," the Mamiya C33 offered a variety of twin-lens assemblies and accessories for every professional need. (That is, and unlike the Rolleiflex, the Mamiya lens assemblies are not permanently mounted and so interchangeable.) Later employed for several famed sea shoots in and around *Apollo* ports of call, the Mamiya C33 is best remembered for the classic LRH self-portraits as Commodore of the Sea Organization. ■

CHAPTER SEVEN

The Photo Shoot
ORGANIZATION

The Photo Shoot
Organization

WHAT BECAME KNOWN AS THE PHOTO SHOOT Organization sprang from a twofold need. First, and following from earlier LRH work on behalf of those local industries and tourist boards, came increasing requests for more. To name but two: a Portuguese winery required operational photographs of

vineyards, cellars and a virtually medieval wine press; while a Caribbean island of Curaçao required shots of holidaymakers for reprint in brochures. To help fulfill such requests, then, came Ron's formation and training of what amounted to a photographic production team. Recruits were drawn from members of a growing *Apollo* crew, and preliminary duties included packing gear, fetching lights and recording results of continuing film/equipment tests. Yet given the second factor behind the forming of a Photo Shoot Organization, those duties soon multiplied.

At issue was an ever-increasing LRH recognition of failing literacy rates among general populations. The subject is vast, involves such matters as a television-hypnotized generation and directly bears upon Ron's development of a broadly exportable study

technology. It further bears upon what he described as a somewhat new photographic art form—namely, the employment of color photograph sequences to convey whole stories without dependence on written words a functionally illiterate reader might not grasp. In essence, then, he described those stories in terms of picture parables, and soon scripted photographic sequences for Scientology instructional materials, books and brochures, as well as broad social awareness campaigns on such societal ills as drug abuse and psychiatry (likewise, subjects pertinent to any discussion of failing literacy rates). As one might imagine, the actual shooting of those scripts proved complex and very similar to movie production, with numerous sets, props, makeup and costumed models. In consequence, we suddenly find L. Ron Hubbard unleashing the whole of his

With Koni Rapid Omega, Fort Charles, Port Royal, Jamaica, 1975

ADVOCATE NEWS

Apollo photographers shooting scenes

The Vincentian

EXPRESS

APOLLO SHOOTS SCENES FOR BROCHURE

Hollywood Director in St. Vincent

AMIGOE

Promotion foto's voor Curaçao

THE NATION

Introducing Ronald Hubbard...

Above
Newspaper articles tell all: "Lafayette Ronald Hubbard, photographer and writer, is engaged in photographic activities which will be taking him around the island"

Right
On Curaçao, 1975, where newspapers further reported, "He has completed the photography for over forty scripts since cruising in the Caribbean"

photographic arsenal—and not merely in terms of cameras and equipment. But rather, here was the man suddenly supervising every aspect of shooting a hundred models in rotation and on ten trucked-in sets.

Newspaper articles tell all: "Lafayette Ronald Hubbard, photographer and writer, is engaged in photographic activities which will be taking him around the island with his well-known *Apollo* photographic team. You can't miss them! Their sets look like something from Columbia or Universal studios with all the professional gear and backdrops." (While to underscore the statement, Ron himself was soon writing of "tourists falling over our tripods.") Of particular interest to those tourists were shots described by Trinidad reporters as historical documentary, e.g., Ron's evening shoot for Scientology's *Advance!* magazine, with an LRH designed and directed Egyptian mummy, replete with mummified (talcum powder) dust. Likewise of interest—and especially so given Ron's employment of some sixty local men, women and children as stand-in models—were shoots of Egyptian scribes and Chinese scholars. Yet most remarked upon, and quite understandably so, was the sheer speed with which Ron managed shoots on those ten rotating sets.

"He has completed the photography for over forty scripts since cruising in the Caribbean," Curaçao papers reported, and described an L. Ron Hubbard arriving on a blacktopped lot to meet a camera crew of fifty and twice as many costumed models. Whereupon he was next seen moving from set to set with astonishing efficiency—quickly calling out for meter reads, exposure settings, filters, lenses and lighting adjustments—before firing with his fully "professional accurateness." Also then inevitably remarked upon were the sheer quantity of shots in the can—seven thousand slides in the space of six weeks—and the veritable industry those slides generated. Indeed, Ron would ultimately employ and direct some four hundred local residents as models and assistants.... All of which, in turn, explains the fully forgivable newspaper headline describing his arrival in a next port of call as "Hollywood Director in St. Vincent."

Above With Mamiya RB67, on location for shooting photo-essays, Curaçao, 1975

Cameras of the Photo Shoot Organization

"He uses as many as four professional cameras at a time…" or so Caribbean journalists reported in the wake of a photo shoot flurry. In fact, however, LRH cameras on those shoots numbered no less than nine, including two Mamiya RB67s, three Koni Rapid Omegas, two Pentax ESs and two Voigtländers. For the record: The Mamiya RB67 and the Koni Rapid Omega are best described as "professional-format" cameras, with sufficiently large negatives for magazine reproduction and interchangeable

Above Ron's professional-format Mamiya RB67s with interchangeable film backs for the shooting of photo-essays

Above With Koni Rapid Omega for magazine covers, Curaçao, 1975   *Above right* Cover for *Advance!* Issue 40

film backs for switching films midroll. The Pentax, with a then newly developed lens "multicoating" for greater clarity and color reproduction, was renowned for providing unusually fine detail in a 35mm format. Also for the record, and as Ron himself would finally remark, these cameras were faithfully rugged—serving equally well from the shimmering heat of those blacktopped, set-filled parking lots to the dim recesses of the New World's oldest synagogue. ∎

Above The Koni Rapid Omegas—professional medium-format cameras—Ron employed for magazine photo shoots

The Lisbon Maritime Museum

NOT LONG AFTER THE FORMATION OF the Photo Shoot Organization (and actually even prior to the formal naming of that team), LRH requests were issued to assistants for biographical summaries of Portuguese explorers. Particularly cited was Vasco da Gama's mapping of a European sea route to Asia along the horn of Africa. Also requested were the visiting hours of a Lisbon Maritime Museum, with most specific questions concerning large-scale models on display, i.e., could one actually board those models?

At issue was a September 1973 appeal from that Lisbon Maritime Museum for an L. Ron Hubbard photo shoot of treasured exhibits—very much including portraits of Vasco da Gama, his early navigational aids, reconstructed maps and scale models of his vessel. If, on the surface, the shoot seems routine, it was not. The Portuguese rightfully take their maritime heritage quite seriously,

and photographing prized artifacts is deemed no casual matter. Indeed, those artifacts were not to be removed from glass display cases, accentuating problems of reflection.

In reply to the problem came Ron's next request: four large sheets of glass and a roll of adhesive tape to fashion a makeshift display case. Then came his call for Rolleiflex, filters and flash lamps, as well as sheets of gauze to soften those lamps. Log notes tell the rest: testing for best angle and distance of lamps from the glass, testing those sheets of gauze and a black backcloth. Notes additionally detail Ron's donning of rubber-soled boots for boarding those models without marring decks and a fully floating shot of Vasco da Gama's flagship actually in the Lisbon estuary:

"Assistant went over the side in diving gear and guided the model on a hidden string. It was shot several ways, mainly against a beautiful cloud effect as the model rose on a high wave.

Above
Lisbon Maritime Museum's model shipbuilder and his scale replica of the LRH flagship, *Apollo*, 1973

Left
With Voigtländer, Portugal, 1973

Left Entrance to Lisbon's Maritime Museum in honor of Portuguese master mariners, 1973

Right
Employing his
Rollei and model
of the Vasco da
Gama flagship,
Ron captured
this shot in
Lisbon's harbor,
1973

A twin-lens reflex (the Rollei) was used to get the lowest possible angle. I hung over the side over the gunwale down to water level and tried to get the model in focus while it wildly swung above in wave and tide. We shot it in color, silhouette and black and white. It was a very difficult trip, actually, shoals, tide, waves, slow launch. But all hands did very well and the four hours afloat were, I hope, well spent by getting a good picture."

Finally, and just for the flavor of the day, there was the LRH request for "two big boxes of bonbons" for two girls who processed the film.

The Synagogue of Mikvé Israel–Emanuel

A S ALSO REPORTED IN A CARIBBEAN press: "Mr. Hubbard has just completed a tourism brochure for the Jewish community..." Specifically, that brochure featured a dozen LRH photographs of what is reputedly the oldest Jewish house of worship in the Americas, the Mikvé Israel–Emanuel Synagogue on the island of Curaçao. Moreover, "[Mr. Hubbard] had already completed an unsolicited historical picture story of the arrival of the original Jews to Curaçao," and so expressed "great interest in photographing the synagogue before he was asked to do the photography work for the brochure." Finally, and quite truthfully: "Some of the most difficult exercises in photography can be found in the synagogue."

Although if the whole truth be told, those difficult exercises arose not from any inherent photographic problem, but from the fact Ron's Mikvé Israel–Emanuel Synagogue shoot

Left Interior of Curaçao's Mikvé Israel–Emanuel, oldest synagogue in the Americas, 1975

Above
Hanukkah oil
menorah dating
from 1715, Mikvé
Israel–Emanuel
Synagogue,
Curaçao, 1975

Right
"The synagogue
interior seen
from the
rear with the
Theba in the
foreground,
looking towards
the Hekhal. The
rabbi preaches
from the small
enclosure in the
center."—LRH

coincided with the Jewish Sabbath. That is, according to Jewish law, no synagogue fixture could be lit on a Saturday.

Several eyewitness accounts tell of Ron pondering the matter—first conferring with Jewish community president Rene Maduro, then stepping to an electric candlelight, unscrewing a bulb and carefully examining the filament. How Ron then replicated that synagogue lighting—whether with modulated strobes reflected off the bulbs, or another means entirely—was not reported. (When later asked, he merely smiled, "Trade secret.") But regardless of technique, those altar lights most definitely seemed to glow. As a matter of fact, when first reviewing Ron's Mikvé Israel–Emanuel photographs, presiding rabbis alarmingly assumed the Sabbath had been broken. Moreover, Ron's shots of those altar lights continue to glow...since the final LRH photographed brochure serves the New World's oldest synagogue to this very day.

On Behalf of the New York Explorers Club

WHILE SUPPLYING HONORED pennants for the likes of Ron's 1940 Alaskan voyage and providing a forum for the likes of astronaut John Glenn, the famed New York Explorers Club also boasts a considerably rich library of journals, accounts and expedition photographs. (After all, what explorer after Ernest Shackleton did not document his journey with a camera?)

To supplement that library, and otherwise on behalf of his most adventurous fellow members, came Ron's Santo Domingo shoot of significant monuments to a man who could not photograph discoveries: Christopher Columbus. Shooting commenced on February 9, 1975, at the Christopher Columbus point of landing with Pentax, Rolleiflex and Koni Rapid Omega. Succeeding shots included the Columbus home, a Plaza de Colón Columbus monument and a cathedral of Santa Maria, reputedly housing the Christopher Columbus tomb.

Also photographed were various views Ron had failed to capture some forty years earlier when high winds off Puerto Rico had shredded the sails of his four-masted schooner and cut short his original Caribbean photographic expedition.

Left Monument to Christopher Columbus, Plaza de Colón, Santo Domingo, Dominican Republic, 1975

Top
Church ruins, Santo Domingo, Dominican Republic, 1975

Bottom
Sanctuary and altar, cathedral of Santa Maria, Santo Domingo, Dominican Republic, 1975

Above Ron's Pentax ES system

The Curaçao Bridge

Among the most acclaimed LRH photographs from Caribbean shoots comes the Queen Juliana Bridge over St. Anna Bay in the Curaçao port of Willemstad. Photographed in May of 1975, the work is especially notable for the fact the bridge is not immediately striking. In point of fact, while the shot has seen reprint in several Scientology publications, and while thousands of Scientologists have regularly caught sight of the Queen Juliana when boarding Scientology's *Freewinds* motor vessel in her home port of Curaçao, rare is the viewer who relates that bridge to what Ron captured with his fisheye lens and Pentax. ■

Right A "fisheye" view of the Queen Juliana Bridge in Willemstad, Curaçao, 1975

Portrait of a
Caribbean Minister

WITH THE GENERAL CIRCULATION OF several hundred frames for Caribbean tourist brochures, Ron inevitably found himself called upon to photograph those who originally commissioned such shoots—most memorably, Curaçao's then Deputy Director of Tourism and Vice Prime Minister, Herman Lichveldt. If later photographs of a delighted minister receiving his portrait effectively conclude the story, a footnote is still in order: Within weeks of the Lichveldt portrait came not only requests for similarly rendered portraits of ministerial colleagues, but promotional posters for tourist board offices and yet another shoot entirely for a Curaçao industry board. ■

Left Willemstad, Curaçao's major port and capital, 1975

CHAPTER EIGHT

FILTERS

Filters

AS OBVIOUSLY REFLECTED IN THE LRH COLLECTION, "I use the living daylights out of filters." Moreover, and more critically, he used those filters with a rare expertise and considered no camera system complete without a corresponding set of filters. Yet to appreciate how he employed his truly considerable filtration arsenal, let us establish a few fundamentals.

While the types of filters are numerous, they generally fall into three categories: filters to correct the appearance of a photograph, filters to enhance a photograph and filters for special effects. Ron employed all, but let us first consider his particular expertise with filters to correct or *compensate* for problems of color rendition.

At the root of such problems lies the fact that color rendition tends to shift depending upon *color temperature*. Color temperature, in turn, essentially refers to the quality of light in terms of color—the reddish light of a sunset registering at one temperature, while blue light on a clear afternoon registers at another. Similarly, lamplight registers at yet another temperature again, as does firelight, fluorescent light and so on. Strictly speaking, then, when discussing color temperature, one is discussing the measurement of the various light rays emanating from a given light source. (See chart on page 181.)

What all this means in terms of filtration is, frankly, a lot. Films are manufactured to best render colors at a specific color temperature and, thus, one sees film for photographing in daylight and others for indoor photographs. The problem is the color of daylight and indoor light are not constant. For instance, an overcast day would measure differently than bright sunlight. The color of light at high altitudes is different than at sea level. The color of light also varies throughout the day, depending upon the position of the sun. And finally—even the color of indoor lighting is variable, what with different types of lights or the typical fluctuations of electrical voltage from AC circuits. While these shifts in the color of light are not so visible to the naked eye, they are very visible to film, which is manufactured to be sensitive to the full spectrum of light. Hence, accuracy of color rendition is greatly

Oporto, Portugal, 1972

affected by these variances in the color of the light exposing the film. As a gross example, any amateur photographer will have noticed that a photograph taken indoors using daylight film, but under the illumination of typical house lamps, will have a yellowish/reddish cast. That is because daylight film is balanced to accurately reproduce colors when illuminated by daylight, which is much bluer than indoor lighting.

That is also why camera flash units put out an illumination of the same color temperature as daylight, thus allowing one to use the same film outdoors or indoors. As another gross example, who hasn't noticed the green tinge on photographs taken under fluorescent lights?

But those are mere examples to illustrate the subject of color temperature for the uninitiated. To a professional, even *slight* variances in color temperature are of concern, as they affect the accurate reproduction of color: meaning, does the photographic image reflect *precisely* the colors of the physical universe one had before his lens?

Color shifts from variations of color temperature can be corrected in processing labs (while computer programs attempt to correct the color of any amateur photograph to look "accurate"). However, an understanding of color temperature basics is fundamental to obtaining the best possible results. Thus, the professional photographer demands accuracy and precision, every step of the way. With color correction, a print made from a negative exposed under lighting conditions not precisely optimized for that film can give a fairly acceptable result. Yet one still has lost something of the full quality possible. The film negative itself has been manufactured to best respond under specific lighting conditions and, where that occurs, no manipulation is required in the lab. That results in the best reproduction possible and, as far as the fully professional photograph, the last word in quality. In essence one is maximizing the result through ensuring that the film is used to its maximum potential by exposing it with the exact color temperature of light for which it was manufactured. Even more to the point, the professional photographer, more often than not, uses *transparency* film (i.e., "slide film") and the photograph in its final form is the image one

Color Temperature

The measurement of color temperature was originally calculated by heating a piece of black carbon until it radiated the various colors of the spectrum and then measuring the temperature of the carbon at those colors. Simply stated, this means that when an object is heated to an appropriate temperature, some of its radiated energy is visible. When metal is gradually heated, the first visible color is "dull cherry red." As the temperature is raised, it visually becomes "orange" and then "yellow" and finally "white" hot. These measurements are known as degrees Kelvin, named for English physicist Lord Kelvin (1824–1907), who devised the scale. (The Kelvin temperatures are the same as Celsius, except the Kelvin scale starts at "absolute zero," the hypothetical temperature at which all molecular activity ceases: -273.16° Celsius.) By way of example, afternoon daylight typically measures 5500° Kelvin, meaning a piece of black carbon heated at 5227° Celsius emits the same light spectrum as that of daylight. Also tungsten light (indoor photoflood lamps) typically measures at 3200° Kelvin.

Color Temperature of Artificial Light	
Match flame	1700K
Candle flame	1850K
Tungsten lamps	
40–100W	2650–2900K
200–500W	2980K
1000W	2990K

Color Temperature of Daylight Light	
Sunlight:	
Sunrise or sunset	2000K
One hour after sunrise	3500K
Early morning, late afternoon	4300K
Average noon (Washington, DC)	5400K
Midsummer	5800K
Overcast sky	6000K
Average summer daylight	6500K
Light summer shade	7100K
Average summer shade	8000K
Partly cloudy sky	8000–10000K

(K = Kelvin)

has on that film when it is developed. Unlike negative film, utilized to print the image on paper, color correction is not possible and the image projected on screen is the final image one gets. Hence, perfect color must be achieved by the photographer when the shutter is snapped, not in the lab.

There is a solution to this problem—an approach directly in line with that LRH emphasis on full technical control across the whole of a photographic line: the color compensation filter. In a word, the color compensation filter allows for minor or major adjustments to obtain precise color rendition under any type of light, and so ensures that very critical matter of photographing what one actually sees through the viewfinder by seeing that the color temperature of light reaching the film and exposing it is exactly that for which the film is best optimized. Most commonly the compensation filter can be employed to adjust the particular color-mix of sunlight at different times of the day. Then, too, the color compensation filter allows for resolving color shifts in the blue light of high altitudes and deep shade, or milky light from airborne dust.

But in any case, we are discussing a photographic tool which returns *control* of color rendering to the photographer himself, and thus a tool Ron embraced to the hilt.

For example: "Calls to the environmental agencies established that the haze was actually not mist but terribly fine particles of dust coming up from the desert areas," he reported, and spoke of working to determine precise combinations of filters for resolving that problem of milky cast from airborne dust. Through the process, he further developed a wholly new means for measuring filters and color temperature with a color temperature meter.

Below
View of Albania from the shores of Corfu, 1968

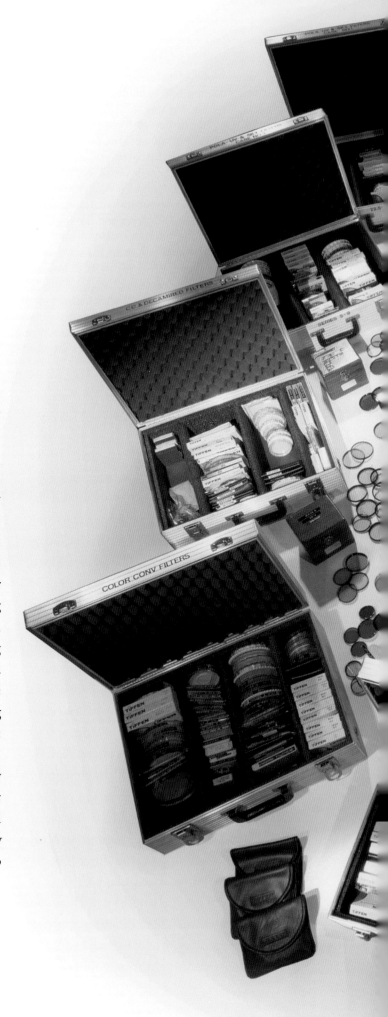

There is more: he would also refine a means for controlling color temperature variations from airborne dust within a studio, and color shifts under studio lights owing to fluctuations in electrical output.

Yet the overriding point is this: with Ron's arsenal of filters working to ensure a consistently precise rendition of color as it actually appeared through the viewfinder, he was then able to create any color he wished... Which is to say, he could just as precisely utilize filters for *enhancing* a photograph—as when turning those "ghastly gray" skies to a vibrant blue on behalf of a Las Palmas tourist board, or washing skies orange for his shots of the Queen Juliana Bridge. Then again, he employed a full range of filters for special effects—as when shooting through a fog filter on Curaçao to replicate the lowland mist of Dutch pastures.

In summation, however, let us simply reiterate that phrase *"I use the living daylights out of filters."* And indeed, while the typical photographer might ultimately collect a few dozen, that LRH arsenal finally comprised no less than 1,304 filters.

The SEI (Salford Electrical Instruments) Meter

WHILE MANY HAVE GLIMPSED photographs of Ron peering through a curious silver-colored cylinder, few have identified that cylinder as the Salford Electrical Instruments meter, or the SEI.

Fewer still appreciate the significance of that meter. For if photography is, indeed, light writing, then here is the instrument Ron selected to write with all possible accuracy. As a word of explanation, he tells us: "The SEI is essentially what is called an 'extinction meter' in that it operates on the principle of making a spot of light disappear in order to get the light level. This is, by the way, the oldest type of light-measuring equipment."

One might further add: When looking through the SEI meter, one sees a spot illuminated by a small electric bulb. The spot is aimed at a "white as white can be" magnesium carbonate target, held in the location where one wants to take his exposure reading. As one turns a rheostat within the dial, that spot grows brighter or dimmer. When the spot finally disappears, the meter is "matched" to the light falling on the target. In other words, that spot is the same brightness as light illuminating the target, and the meter is now providing a direct and exact measurement of the light intensity of the subject one wishes to expose. By simply consulting exposure scales on the body of the meter, one then sets the correct exposure settings on one's camera.

In the same way, one can aim the spot on distant targets for measuring reflected light from subjects impossible to approach for close readings—inaccessible mountain peaks, for example. (Hence, Ansel Adams's employment of the very same meter to formulate his famed system of photographic exposure control for mountain landscapes.)

Then again, whereas many other types of meters do not accurately measure extreme areas of light or dark, the SEI provides consistent measurement across a broad range of bright and low light. In an age before computerized meters, then, the SEI provided the ultimate.

For these reasons, the SEI occupied a significant place within Ron's photographic

One sees a small spot illuminated by a small electric bulb. (See Figure 1.) As one turns the base of the meter, the spot grows brighter or dimmer. (See Figures 1 and 3.) When the spot finally disappears (Figure 2), the meter is matched to the amount of light falling on the subject.

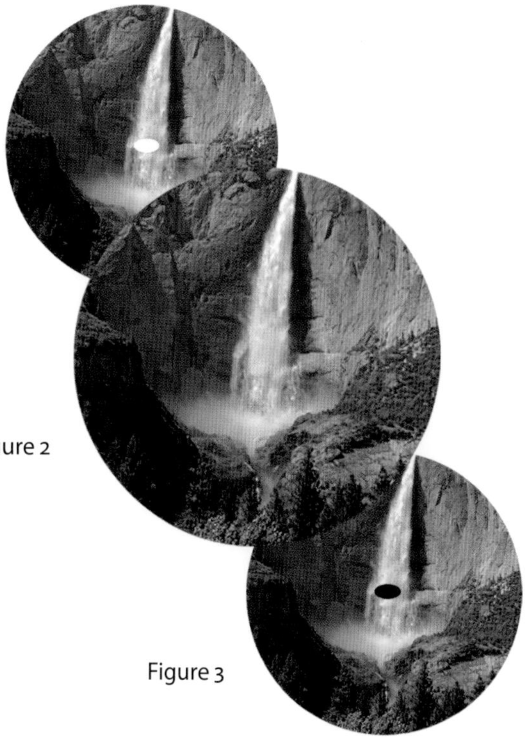

Figure 1

Figure 2

Figure 3

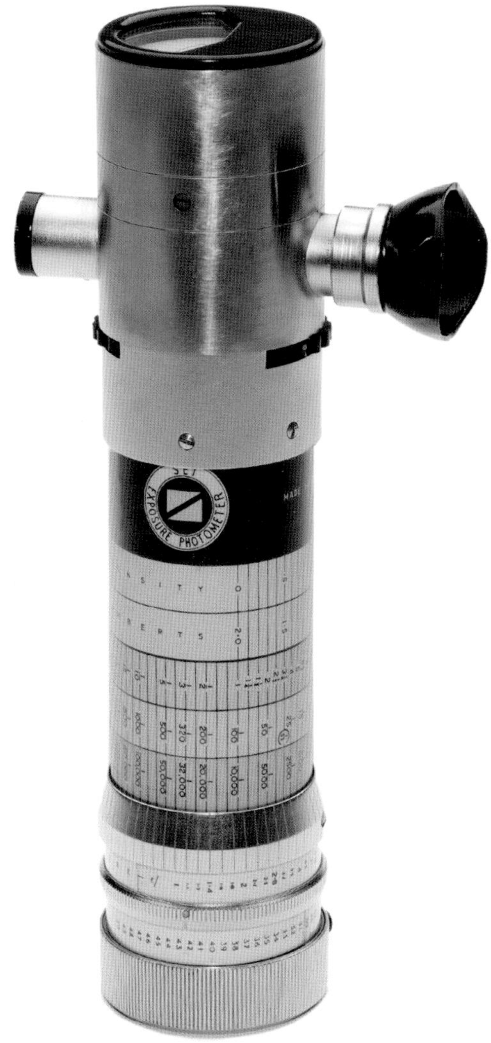
EXPOSURE PHOTOMETER

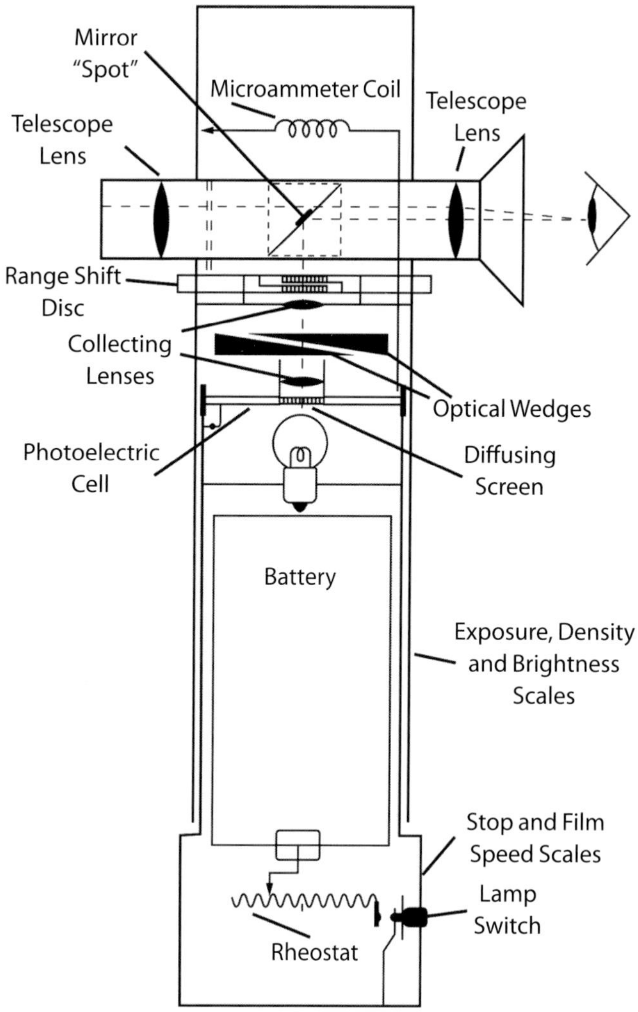
Mirror "Spot"
Microammeter Coil
Telescope Lens
Telescope Lens
Range Shift Disc
Collecting Lenses
Optical Wedges
Photoelectric Cell
Diffusing Screen
Battery
Exposure, Density and Brightness Scales
Stop and Film Speed Scales
Lamp Switch
Rheostat

A cutaway illustration of the SEI meter showing its internal workings

Right
The SEI light
meter served
Ron as the
instrument
against which
he calibrated
all other light
meters

arsenal for more than three decades—or when he first employed the meter in a London darkroom to measure light levels for photographic printing. (The procedure, incidentally, was altogether inventive and so finally dubbed "The Hubbard Method.") Latterly, because the SEI may be calibrated for pinpoint accuracy in any location or light level, the meter also served Ron as the instrument against which he calibrated all other meters... Which is to say, here was the *standard* for truly precision light measurement and for *that* reason, when Salford Electrical Instruments finally closed its doors and ceased production in 1982, Ron went so far as to purchase all calibration equipment and rights, maintained to this day by those he trained in its use. ▪

Ron's desert estate in La Quinta, California, where he codified
all photographic fundamentals between 1977 and 1979

CHAPTER NINE

The LATTER YEARS

The Latter Years

WITH A RETURN TO THE UNITED STATES IN 1975, AND eventual resettlement in California, came what may be regarded as the singularly most significant years of Ron's photographic career. For quite in addition to continual shooting across three divergent landscapes, these years saw his final codification of all

photographic fundamentals—literally from shutter click to final print. But to focus as Ron himself first focused, let us consider his shoots.

Those shoots were initially conducted near the Southern California desert community of Palm Springs, where Ron first established a cinematographic unit for the production of Scientology training films. And while the greater part of his film and camera expertise was now devoted to production of those instructional films, he nonetheless continued his still photography work to illustrate Scientology instructional materials, brochures and posters (by way of example, his poster for the LRH drug and toxin detoxification method known as the Purification Rundown program). As earlier, photographs were meticulously planned and executed on either sets or location, which, in turn, necessitated

much photographic testing in the face of continually advancing film lines, processes and equipment. Moreover, between intense bouts of production on those Scientology films, he carried on shooting stills for the sheer love of still photographs—as when calling for a still camera when catching sight of an especially spectacular sun and cloud effect on a cine location. Then again, as previously mentioned, it was further here Ron packed his holstered Minox and a Minolta CLE for those ultra "real life" candids of shoppers between vegetable bins in an Alpha Beta supermarket.

While completion of outstanding cine projects freed Ron from day-to-day demands of cinematographic production, his schedule still allowed little time for photography. Rather, he could now more fully devote himself to Scientology research, and he did just that.

Southern California, 1979

Above A selection of Ron's "real life" photographs in local food supermarkets, Riverside County, 1979

The Minox

"You wouldn't think anything so small was such a big subject!" In fact, however, the subminiature Minox carries a considerably long and intriguing history. Originally of Russian design, and actually issued to Soviet spies through the Second World War, the Minox has always possessed real mystique. Moreover, with an LRH designed and custom-manufactured holster, the Minox became the last word in utterly unobtrusive shooting, e.g., when later residing in Southern California and experimenting with candid photography in the manner of famed French photographer Henri Cartier-Bresson, Ron employed camera and holster for snapping "real life" photographs of shoppers in a local supermarket. Then, too, as Ron concluded, when discussing the Minox, one is speaking of "a very cute camera indeed." ■

Minolta CLE

If, as Ron declared, no photographer should ever find himself without camera, then here was the fully portable but no less professional solution: a Leica-designed Minolta Compact Leica Electronic (CLE). While the Minolta may resemble an inexpensive point-and-shoot, it is not. With utterly precision operation and a Leitz lens from the famed Leica factory, this was most definitely a professional camera.

As with the Minox, Ron carried the Minolta in a holster of his own design. As a matter of fact, camera and holster were virtually always on his belt; for as the story goes, that Minolta actually followed from the evening he attended the birth of a colt in his Creston stables…and, to be sure, found himself admiring a magnificent newborn without a camera. ■

In 1945, while en route to Los Angeles from Oakland's Oak Knoll Naval Hospital, LRH composed the watercolor of Saint Anne's Church. Upon his return, in the early 1980s, he photographed the very same scene.

He additionally authored such milestone works as his nonreligious moral code, *The Way to Happiness*. While with what little spare time he had on his hands, Ron celebrated his fiftieth anniversary as an author with the writing of eleven *New York Times* bestsellers—*Battlefield Earth* and the ten-volume *Mission Earth* series. Eventually, however, and also through the course of ongoing Scientology research, Ron found the time to travel...and with that travel, we come to his next field of photographic focus: the central California mother lode country and original site of the California gold rush.

A landscape he had known from youth, the mother lode country had also served as a brief resting point en route to Los Angeles from Oakland's Oak Knoll Naval Hospital, remembered today as a site of critical Dianetics research. Yet when initially passing through a historically rich Columbia mining town, he carried no camera and so recorded impressions of the Saint Anne's Church and cemetery in a watercolor. (His vintage Cadillac also carried no air-conditioning unit, and so he rigged a cooling device with blocks of ice below the air vent.) Upon his return in the early 1980s—this time aboard a customized Blue Bird motor home—he carried both medium-format and 35mm systems. Literally retracing his footsteps, then, he shot what he had sketched so many years earlier.

Gadget Bag

If experienced photographers will frequently fill camera bags with gadgets for a quick repair or tricky shot, here is the carefully itemized LRH gadget bag. As a word of explanation, Ron succinctly defined that gadget bag in terms of those "odds and ends" unforeseen circumstances might require. Or more precisely: "Those things necessary to repair the camera, such as a screwdriver and pliers, lens paper and other accessories to clean the camera and any other necessary item for that shoot (i.e., you might need some tape if you are doing light tests)." Among the less obvious contents: thumbtacks for securing

backdrops or testing patterns, clothespins for securing a model's costume, pocket level for leveling tripod and camera. Also, perhaps not immediately self-explanatory, but nonetheless essential, was the stopwatch for timing long exposures—as when Ron found himself in the dead of a Curaçao night for what he described as an "industrial weirdo" shot of a distant oil refinery. Finally, and as a last word on the photographer who is indeed fully prepared for any eventuality, one finds the Skol suntan lotion for protection from the desert sun and snakebite kit for rattlesnake-infested desert trails. ■

Finally, resettling on the several hundred acres of his Creston, California, ranch come Ron's photographs from shoots presented here.

Typically, those shoots commenced at one o'clock in the afternoon, between hours of Scientology research. Equipment included newly advanced 35mm cameras, tripod and accessories carefully packed in a four-wheel-drive Subaru pickup—or, if on foot, camera around his neck and camera bag on the shoulder of an assistant. Again, however, one is speaking of somewhat less formal work. For with others now successfully shooting the bulk of shots required for Scientology materials, Ron no longer found it necessary to immerse himself in the daily production of such photographs. And so, as a consummate photographer is forever working to sharpen his skills, Ron now took the opportunity to do just that: the continued honing of photographic skills. For example, many a shot was actually conceived when examining photographs presented in the *Kodak Library of Creative Photography* series, and particularly a volume entitled *Capture the Beauty in Nature*. That is, and expressly as photographic exercise, he would select a particular photograph from the text, scout out a similar subject or scene and shoot. In precisely that manner came many a shot of what the text described as "patterns in nature," including extreme close-ups of tree bark and Ron's still life of a rose, presented here. Then, too, while a chapter on wildlife photography provided a shot of a timber wolf balefully glancing to the cameraman's lens, Ron managed to coax the very same pose from a Creston ranch dog.

Also the site of numerous shoots through the 1980s was the lily-pond home of ducks, swans and an especially photogenic heron dubbed Audrey. (Although as a word of advice to a student-cum-assistant, who continually found herself shooting a fleeing Audrey, Ron spoke of first shooting wildlife from a distance, then slowly stepping in, still shooting, for the ideal frame.) Also from these days were continual shoots along the hundred-plus acres of Creston pastures—the domain of thoroughbreds, quarter horses, buffalo and even llamas. Indeed, so regularly did Ron shoot from those pastures, thoroughbreds would habitually flock to that approaching Subaru, intent on the carrots or sugar he carried in his windbreaker pockets.

If not germane to any single shot from these days, we further come to a most telling story from the Creston carpenter who helped erect the pristine white fences across that pastureland. Noting Ron on daily inspection rounds with a clearly professional 35mm camera habitually at

his chest, the carpenter eventually requested a recommendation of an inexpensive first camera. Ron, in reply, asked for a day to consider the matter. Whereupon, he returned the following afternoon to present that carpenter with a perfect first camera. If an altogether simple story, the point is nonetheless important: Ron eagerly helped anyone who also wished to write with light.

Finally, there is all else Ron's final photographs tell us about a man who just simply loved photography. Which is to say, here were a full five thousand frames from continual shooting, day in, day out. ■

Left and above
Three in a series of photographs along Ron's Creston, California, pastures, conceived when examining shots from the *Kodak Library of Creative Photography* series

The 35mm Systems

While Ron long favored larger-format cameras, by the 1970s he was also seriously examining, testing and then regularly shooting with the Olympus OM—a 35mm pro-line camera system offering a wide array of interchangeable lenses and attachments. Lightweight and dependable, with consistently faithful metering across a wide range of lighting situations, Ron would eventually dub his first OM "Old Workhorse."

With the advent of new plastics, metal alloys, microprocessor circuitry and microelectronics through the early 1980s, Ron next turned to those camera systems of the advanced 35mm revolution still unfolding to this day. To an LRH who had previously witnessed some sixty years of photographic change—from dry plates to roll film, from monochromatic to color and more—that 35mm revolution was nonetheless intriguing. Indeed,

Above Ron's Olympus OM system, a professional-line 35mm camera offering a wide array of interchangeable lenses and attachments

many a spare moment at his Creston, California, ranch found him leafing through pages of a *Popular Photography* or *Modern Photography* for notices on those newly unfolding 35mm pro-line systems.

He eventually examined and tested them all—scores of cameras, lenses and professional attachments, and six complete systems. Moreover, he frequently tested those systems within days or weeks of manufacturer's release. Typically, that

testing was meticulous—from exposure, metering and mechanical action to the placement of controls and image clarity on all lenses comprising the camera system. ■

Above Ron fully tested all elements and functions of the Nikon F system, including the Nikon F3AF—the first professional autofocus camera released by Nikon

Leica

As a broad word on the series Ron finally declared the best, he described the Leica as the "great-grandfather of all 35mm cameras" (in reference to the fact Leica virtually invented the 35mm still camera). Testing commenced in late 1982 when, following his review of lesser systems, he called for the ultimate... and, indeed, "I've never seen anything shoot pictures like those Leicas."

In a clear statement of feelings for the world-renowned Leica lens system stands an LRH collection that is exceedingly large—from the smallest micro lens capable of shooting the head of a fly to the long lens and telephoto. As a matter of fact, so significant a Leica user was Ron, distributors finally presented him with a limited edition Leica display case...of which Ron remarked, "Someday this will be in a museum." And he was right. For along with all other cameras featured through these pages, that case and Leica R4 reside today in the LRH camera room. ■

Right Ron's extensive Leica 35mm collection includes the Leica R4. He describes the Leica as the "great-grandfather" of all 35mm cameras.

FLASH SYSTEM FLASH GUNS POLAROID CAMERAS LINHOF LINHOF GRAFLEX

LIGHT METERS VOIGTLÄNDER OLYMPUS NIKONOS MINOX MAMIYA RB67

CANON NIKON LEICA MINOLTA CLE

The Camera Room

containing the complete collection of L. Ron Hubbard's camera and photographic equipment

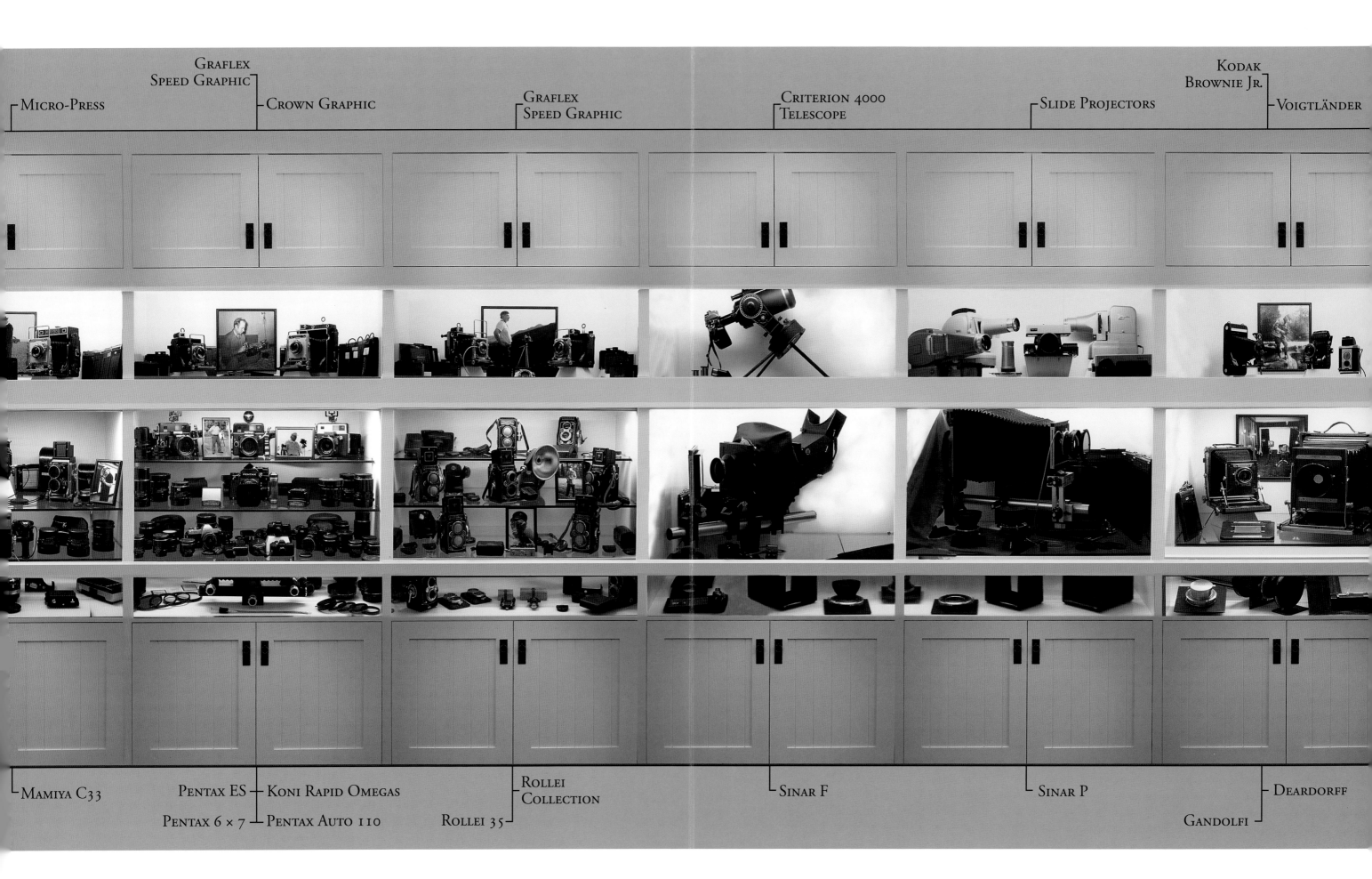

GRAFLEX
SPEED GRAPHIC

KODAK
BROWNIE JR.

MICRO-PRESS   CROWN GRAPHIC   GRAFLEX
SPEED GRAPHIC   CRITERION 4000
TELESCOPE   SLIDE PROJECTORS   VOIGTLÄNDER

MAMIYA C33   PENTAX ES — KONI RAPID OMEGAS   ROLLEI
COLLECTION   SINAR F   SINAR P   DEARDORFF

PENTAX 6 × 7 — PENTAX AUTO 110   ROLLEI 35   GANDOLFI

Testing

I F A PHOTOGRAPH ULTIMATELY FOLLOWS from an interconnection of camera, lens, film, meter, lights and darkroom procedure, then technical excellence follows from a technically flawless performance of each component. To ensure that technical perfection—from shutter click to final print—photographic technicians have devised all manner of testing procedures. While those procedures are frequently complex, it is something of an LRH hallmark to simplify and codify the fundamentals of any endeavor—very much including the testing of every component in that photographic line from camera to print.

The operative word is *every* component— every camera, lens, meter, lamp, strobe and type of film. All were exactingly tested to pinpoint the accuracy of, and optimum performance level for, any single component and any combination of components. But for a sense of just how exacting was that scrutiny, let us consider an LRH test of film.

"No new film may be put on a production line until fully tested," he declared, and here the operative word is *fully*. That is, every factor relative to film behavior was both separately and rigorously tested. Ron tested to determine a film's sensitivity to light. He tested to determine film contrast; how much a film can be overexposed and underexposed; and for color balance to determine best color reproduction. Moreover, each test was most precise. The first test, for example, the test of a film's sensitivity to light, or its "speed," essentially requires shooting rolls of film against a test pattern of progressively darker shades from white to black. The film is shot in such a way as to reveal its extremes of performance relative to light. One then isolates the frame reproducing the most tones of the test pattern. In other words, the film is shot to determine the exact amount of light required to consistently produce a negative which faithfully reproduces the tones of a scene.

As a further note on analyzing test results, a word is in order on the acquired darkroom skill of "reading" negatives. Oftentimes photographers will view their test results on a print made from the test negative. While *the method* is useful in seeing how one's final photograph will look when printed, it enters the variable of how the lab manipulates the print and can be misleading as regards how the negative itself is reacting. The fact is, Ron could read a test negative, or any negative for that matter, and immediately determine what had happened to that negative—whether ever so slightly overexposed or underexposed, overdeveloped or underdeveloped, and its accuracy of color.

He could further, and likewise immediately, determine the best means of printing that negative... and on what type of paper. Then again, for really narrowing down the one and only optimum level of film performance as regards to light sensitivity, he devised his own means of analyzing grain particles in film. Which is to say, he was reading negatives to obtain what one is ultimately testing for—the perfect negative.

The LRH test for film contrast is no less exacting, and requires that one shoots faces of people beside test patterns on several easels—each person and easel is precisely set at receding intervals from the camera and under *very* precise lighting. Tests to determine best color reproduction require the shooting of several film rolls against a myriad of different colors and contrasts of lighting, and then closely monitoring how the lab processes each roll. If for any reason one changes labs, various tests must be repeated. Then, too, because the various factors relative to film behavior may slightly vary from one batch of film to the next, Ron subjected every new batch of film to tests. In similar ways, Ron developed tests to eliminate

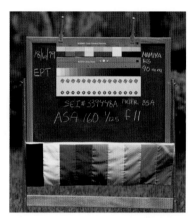

variables of lens performance and clarity, including minute variables of exactly how much light passes through a lens at any given lens setting. Then again, he developed tests to eliminate variables of camera shutter speeds, intensities of strobe light output and light meter performance. Finally, as noted, tests for equipment and film were conducted in combination to pinpoint the *ideal* combination. Again, the net result is a technical command of all factors requisite to getting that shot a photographer originally envisions. Or even more fundamentally: here is yet another means to ensure that when writing with light, the intended message is indeed *communicated*.

While the history of LRH testing procedures is extensive—records actually tell of Ron testing film and camera performance as early as 1932—his dedication to the subject is probably best exemplified by what he passed on to his students. When those students purchased new stocks of film or acquired new cameras, the first images recorded were the testing patterns mounted on a chalkboard for determining ideal exposure, color reproduction, focus and more. ■

CHAPTER TEN

INSTRUCTION

Instruction

IF, AS RON SO FAMOUSLY DECLARED, "ART IS A WORD WHICH summarizes THE QUALITY OF COMMUNICATION," then it logically follows that a quality photograph must, above all, communicate. Yes, photography involves the technical rendering of a shot—with film, lens, aperture and shutter speed—but as Ron also declared, the technical

rendition is *always* subordinate to the resultant communication. In that regard, the photographer is ultimately engaged in the realm of art and the field of communication, and the quality photograph is just as ultimately all about a picture that "talks."

The statement is crucial and says everything about what Ron imparted to photographic students, beginning in late 1978. For here was not a course in photographic technique, but the bottom-line fundamentals behind that dictum: "First and foremost is the subject of message. You have to make a shot *talk*." Then, too, here was photography defined exclusively in terms of communication, and so expressly concerned with the question: "What is this picture I am looking at saying?" Moreover, here was a view of all photographic technicalities as ultimately following from making those

pictures *talk*. Which is to say, when discussing questions of lenses, apertures and shutter speeds, one is finally and only discussing tools for photographic *communication*.

In emphasis of the statement, students were purposely equipped with what was then the simplest of cameras, the Kodak Instamatic. The reasoning was simple: because the Instamatic offered no shutter or aperture control, nor even control of the focus, students could not rely on technical wizardry to accomplish their shots. Or as Ron himself explained, the cameras "have no particular virtue except they are largely automatic and one wanted the student to get his attention on the pictures and what he was taking, rather than on his camera." Moreover, as he elsewhere added: "You can't pass up a shot just because you haven't got a special lens. You try to get the shot with the lens you have got.

Pastureland, Sussex, England, 1964

Above
Hundreds of LRH
instructional
critiques
provided a
wealth of
practical tips in
making a picture
talk

You will often find yourself on location without that special piece of equipment that has never been built and you will have to make up for it with your own ingenuity."

Thus equipped with what amounted to the irreducible minimum of a camera, students were required to make each shot talk with the irreducible minimum of photographic basics—not shutter speed and aperture control—but the bottom-line fundamentals of photographic communication, i.e., framing and composition. While as a particularly key word on those fundamentals, Ron further declared:

"There are only a few basics in composing pictures. The difference between a professional photographer and an amateur is detectable by anyone at a glance even when they don't know why.

"An amateur, for some reason, tries to get the most possible into one frame. He also does not see the world, from a photographic viewpoint, with a frame around it. He does not fill the frame. And he does not delete unwanted things.

"A professional on the other hand is highly selective as to the center of interest. He excludes out—deletes—everything that does not pertain to the message. And he sees objects with a frame around them. And, aside from composure and finishing quality, that is what separates the amateurs from the professionals, just the items in this paragraph and no others."

Armed with rolls of black and white film in those fixed-focus, point-and-shoot cameras, students pursued a variety of shots, from portraits of residents in a neighboring community to come what may in immediately surrounding hills, e.g., "Later that day I was on a mountain canyon trail and came upon a snake in the path. After seeing that it was harmless and didn't seem to be going anywhere, I got down on the ground about two feet away, and snapped off three shots. Then I picked him up to pose him in a nice spot, but he wasn't at all for it and so I let him go." If students were initially hesitant to submit shots as not "good enough," Ron vehemently encouraged otherwise. Photographs, with explicit shot notations and student remarks, were then submitted by the hundreds, and Ron replied with instructional critiques, e.g., "Your criticism is unjustified. This is a case where all of that inclusion—as opposed to deletion—tells you that this is a person and that he is out in a wide countryside and that he is in an enclosure and that he is looking for something."

In pace with student improvement, and that pace was remarkably rapid, LRH instructional critiques further provided a wealth of practical tips, all eventually published for the benefit of later students and still, of course, studied to this day.

Once a student had mastered those fundamentals of framing and composition, he was ready to acquire skills of technical rendition. That is, he was ready to instill a sense of motion with slower shutter speeds or freeze the action with faster shutter speeds. He was ready to learn how to emphasize key points of interest with selective focus or through different lens aperture settings. Or even more to the point, having mastered the fundamental concept that a good picture is one that communicates—a picture that talks—he could now master the technicalities of a camera with the full understanding of their purpose and use—to help make a picture *talk*. And here again, Ron worked to codify the technical aspects of photography, distilling them down to the basics, such that anyone could learn and apply them.

As Ron explained, there were certain irreducible fundamentals to employing a camera, and a critical sequence to taking any shot. Or once again, more simply, there was what he described in terms of "Camera Stable Data." The phrase is fully descriptive. To every separate sector of artistic endeavor, he tells us, there are the rules—the stable data, the senior data. "We don't follow the rules because we're told to; we follow the rules to get a product that is effective and brings about what we want brought about." Consequently, and regardless of discipline: "You have to sort out what the senior data are—the rules—and know them cold, so you don't even have to think about them and can think with them."

As we have seen, sorting out those rules from a vast and sometimes daunting body of photographic data and lore proved no small task—consumed no small quantity of film, involved no small measure of research, testing and codification. Yet the fact remains, when photographic students embarked upon that LRH instructional program, they effectively received a lesson from some sixty years of light writing. For it was expressly on behalf of those students that Ron originally codified the senior data—the rules. ▪

What defines effective composition, whether photographic or otherwise? How is one to recognize it, utilize it and perfect it for the improvement of any photograph or visual rendering? These are the questions addressed and resolved with what Ron provided his students in late 1979, and what is presented here.

Behind what Ron so succinctly delineates stands a considerably long and involved study. As a matter of fact, one finds LRH notes on compositional theory from as early as 1938—or from discussions with Matty Mathieu, remembered today from the pages of ART as that "dear friend" and New York portraitist, expounding upon abstract theory. Then again, Saint Hill Manor bookshelves were amply stocked with texts on the subject; while by April of 1979, he was reviewing yet another series of standard texts on composition. Whereupon we come to the LRH notes originally provided to photographic students who might have otherwise found themselves snarled in those texts. Needless to say, when discussing composition, one is speaking of an absolutely integral factor to the meaningful photograph or, for that matter, any visual form with which one wishes to communicate a message.

NOTES ON COMPOSITION

by L. RON HUBBARD

P EOPLE REMAIN PRETTY FOGGY on this subject of composition. There is an omitted definition in English for *composition* that has apparently also been omitted for the last X-thousand years on this planet, which is that "composition is the arrangement of objects and people in the scene to forward the message."

Lacking that, they have gone into all sorts of stylized nonsense and have made it seem a very difficult subject. There are formal conventional ways of composing things and these too have to be known as they often will forward a message quite rapidly. But, the people who invented them didn't actually work it out from that point of view.

The silliest one of the lot is this fulcrum and balance factor, where the little object must be a long distance and the big object a short distance. This mechanical composition is what is kept foremost in mind by most artists and it makes their pictures trite and stupid-looking.

So there's lots of false data in this field of composition. That is probably what has it bogged down. *Ron*

Approaching Saint Hill Manor, 1964

As we have said, the first and foremost emphasis of all LRH photographic instruction lay with those irreducible fundamentals. That is, what comprises the irreducible minimum for any respectable photograph? What must every serious student minimally master, every professional routinely perform and every amateur likewise apply to improve any photograph?

The answer is L. Ron Hubbard's "Camera Stable Data."

As noted, the title is entirely descriptive. From an esoteric world of coveted technique and perplexing theory comes the bottom-line steps for elevating any shot into a realm of quality work. Or once again, more simply: here are the checklisted basics of better photography LRH students literally carried in hand as they set out for a shoot. Because here is what a lifelong and consummate photographer wished to impart to anyone, experienced and inexperienced alike, who would likewise write with light.

CAMERA STABLE DATA

by L. RON HUBBARD

Checklist

0. KNOW your CAMERA and FILM and LIGHTING by study and drilling and the film's reaction to various lights as well as lighting.

1. PRECONCEIVE THE PICTURE YOU ARE GOING TO SHOOT.

   a. Alternate: Recognize a picture and take it. Reduce the comm lag between seeing a picture and taking it. When you have control of subject and lighting or can assert control (such as time of day, position of things at different times), recognize that you *will* have a picture if you preconceive and plan it. When you just plain *see* a picture, reduce the time of recognizing it and getting it on the film by properly following the remaining steps with lightning speed. Pictures don't wait. Two or three seconds or less and they can be gone.

2. Go there or set it up.

3. MAKE THE PICTURE TALK.

4. COMPOSE.

   a. THE FORMAL RULES OF COMPOSITION ARE FOLLOWED.

   b. You don't have lines going through the back of the person's head.

   c. There are no poles or wires or unsightly objects between you and the picture or the subject and the background.

   d. You haven't split the interest.

   e. You don't have a littered, messed-up background or foreground.

5. FRAME IT. (Include the wanted, exclude the unwanted.) (Carry out your composition planning.)

Ron's Gandolfi

6. Get the camera settings right for the film, S (Shutter), A (Aperture), F (Focus), E (Exposure), (SAFE).

7. FILL THE FRAME with the set or view or characters or objects. (If not, go back and recompose.)

8. MAKE SURE THINGS ARE RECOGNIZABLE TO THE VIEWER WITHOUT ANY SOUND TRACK OR EXPLANATION SO HE KNOWS WHAT HE IS LOOKING AT.

9. CENTER THE ACTION—keeping in mind composition.

This isn't really training still photography, but cinematography. You can, however, do this with a still camera.

Double rainbow over harbor entrance to Kontokali, Corfu, Greece, 1968

Self-portrait, Creston, California, 1985

One Last Image

This is the attitude you must have.

"I'm the photographer.

I'm the person who's going to shoot this picture.

This picture is going to do you a lot of good.

When I shoot them, they're good."

Make sure that your line is sufficiently letter-perfect

so that when you click the shutter,

it's in the can.

L. Ron Hubbard

APPENDIX

Glossary | 231
Index | 259

GLOSSARY

A

Ability: a magazine of Dianetics and Scientology, issued from March 1955, containing informative technical material, programs and other items of interest to Dianeticists and Scientologists. Page 68.

Adams, Ansel: (1902–1984) American photographer, known for his black and white photographs of wilderness areas of the American West. He worked to establish the importance of the field of photography with images that convey both the vast scale and the intimate detail of a landscape. Page 124.

Agadir: a seaport on the Atlantic Ocean, located in southwestern Morocco. Agadir's large natural harbor makes it one of the principal ports of Morocco. Page 145.

Agat: a village on the southwest coast of the island of Guam. Page 17.

Agfa: the name of a German company that originated as a chemical manufacturing firm in the 1860s and began making cameras in the mid-1920s. One early model of Agfa cameras was a type that folded out to take a picture. The lens was positioned at the end of a bellows, which would flatten into the case when the camera was closed up and then extend outward when the case was opened. Page 29.

air meet: a gathering of people taking part in or viewing aerial sporting activities. The word *meet* means a sports gathering of competitive events. Air meets involve activities such as air racing and aerobatics, with competitors being judged on style, accuracy, speed, altitude, etc., and have been popular since the early 1900s, when the airplane was invented. Page 3.

airstrip: a small landing field having only one runway. Page 38.

Albania: a small, mountainous country in southeastern Europe. Albania lies on the *Adriatic Sea,* an arm of the Mediterranean Sea, east of Italy. Page 181.

Alpha Beta: a chain of supermarkets with locations throughout California, until being sold to other chains in the late 1900s. The chain started (1915) with one store that used a self-service system of arranging groceries in alphabetical order and, by 1917, the name Alpha Beta had come into use. Page 191.

Anglo-gone-somewhat-native: an English-speaking person in a place where English is not the language of the majority, who has adopted aspects of the culture of the place he now lives in. Page 17.

aperture: the opening in a camera that controls the amount of light passing through the lens and onto the film. Page 217.

Apollo: from the late 1960s through the mid-1970s, the upper-management activities for all Churches of Scientology over the world were conducted from a fleet of ships, the main vessel being the *Apollo.* The 350-foot (110-meter) vessel also served as Mr. Hubbard's home and center for his many research activities. Page 3.

ASA: (as noted on the photographic testing board) *ASA* stands for *American Standards Association,* an organization of American industry and business groups dedicated to the development of trade and communication standards. The *ASA number* is a designation for *film speed,* the sensitivity of a film to light. A fast film (for example, with an ASA number of 200 or higher) is more sensitive to light and needs less exposure. A slow film (for example, with an ASA number of 80 or lower) is not so sensitive to light and needs more exposure. Page 213.

Asiatic Fleet: one of the three fleets that the United States naval forces were divided into during the early and mid-twentieth century. The Asiatic Fleet was mostly in the Philippines. Page 17.

auditing: the application of Dianetics and Scientology processes to a person. A *process* is a set of questions asked or directions given by an auditor to help a person find out things about himself or life and to improve his condition. Also called *processing.* Page 65.

Auditor, The: a magazine created by L. Ron Hubbard in 1964 and sent out regularly from Saint Hill to swiftly carry information on his latest technical developments as well as news of Saint Hill. (An *auditor* is a Dianetics or Scientology practitioner. The word *auditor* means one who listens; a listener.) Page 65.

Austin: any of several vehicles manufactured by the Austin Motor Company of Great Britain, a company founded in 1905 by engineer Herbert Austin (1866–1941), who designed and built some of the first automobiles in the country. Page 131.

available: natural or usual light, as in sunlight and lamplight, used in taking a photograph (rather than with special lighting equipment). Page 101.

B

back(s): also called *film back,* on some cameras, the rear panel of the camera, which includes the film. A film back of one camera is often interchangeable with another camera. One common use is to put a Polaroid back on another camera. Since the Polaroid back contains film that develops instantly, a shot can be taken of a given scene to determine beforehand the effects of flash lighting, etc. Page 99.

baleful(ly): harmful or threatening harm or evil. Page 198.

barnstorming: in the early days of aviation, touring (the country) giving short airplane rides, exhibitions of stunt flying, etc. This term comes from the use of barns as hangars. Page 1.

batting off: doing something with great speed. Page 3.

bearing mention: calling for or requiring a statement about something. Page 1.

bears upon: relates to or affects something. Page 157.

beehive safelights: a *safelight* is a type of light used in darkrooms that filters out the rays that are harmful to sensitive film and photographic paper. A beehive safelight was so named due to its resemblance to the domed shape of a beehive. Page 91.

benchmark: pertaining to or used as a standard of excellence, achievement, etc., against which anything similar must be measured or judged. Page 2.

better part of, the: the larger part of something. Page 11.

big top: the largest or main tent (top) of a circus. Page 3.

billibutugun: a musical instrument of Guam, consisting of a long stick with a string stretched between its two ends. Near the center is a resonator, such as a cocoanut, which is placed on the stomach. Page 22.

bleachers: a section of cheaper seats, usually bare benches in tiers, often without a roof, for spectators at outdoor sporting events. Page 136.

blessings: approval or good wishes. Page 141.

blue flash: a reference to photographic flashbulbs designed to produce a flash of blue-white light of a color similar to daylight and producing a similar effect in the resultant color photograph. This blue color was originally achieved by coating a normally clear flashbulb (that emitted a whiter light) with a layer of blue plastic. Page 100.

boot: a space at the back of a car for carrying luggage. Page 87.

bottom-line: characterized as being the basic aspect of something. Page 217.

box camera: a simple camera consisting of a rigid box and a fixed simple lens. Page 9.

bridle path: a path for riding horses, not wide enough for vehicles. Page 37.

British Colour Council: an industry-standards organization that published indexes of named colors for use by British government, industry, academia and horticulture from the 1930s through the 1960s. Page 85.

British Columbia: a province in western Canada on the Pacific coast. Page 51.

brush hook: also called *bush hook,* a tool with a curved blade and long handle used to cut bushes. Page 58.

C

cable release: a flexible wire that is pressed at one end to activate a camera shutter. Page 101.

Camp Parsons: a Boy Scout camp located in Washington State, in the northwestern United States. Page 6.

candid: relating to photography that shows subjects acting in a natural, informal way without being posed or rehearsed. Page 2.

can, in the: recorded on film; completed. From the metal container used for storing film. Page 158.

Canon: a Japanese camera first produced by the Kwanon (later Canon) company in the mid-1930s, with a popular single-lens reflex model introduced in the late 1950s. Over the years, Canon has expanded to become a multinational manufacturer of optical products and business equipment. Page 72.

Cape Chacon: the southeastern point of Prince of Wales Island, Alaska. Ketchikan is further north, on an adjacent island. Page 55.

Capitol Building: the white-marble, domed building in Washington, DC, where the United States Congress meets. *Congress* is the lawmaking body of the United States Government. Page 12.

carabao: a water buffalo that is native to Southeast Asia. Large, gentle animals with horns, they have been used on farms, as for plowing fields, pulling wagons and the like. Page 20.

Cartier-Bresson, Henri: (1908–2004) French photographer, best known for his spontaneous photographs that helped establish photojournalism as an art form. Page 192.

cast about: look around for something. Page 12.

catch as catch can: using any method or means available or that can be applied. Page 37.

"cathedral lighting effect": the slanting rays of light which, coming through clouds, resemble the rays coming through the upper windows of a cathedral and slanting down into the interior of the building. Page 147.

Cedar of Lebanon: a type of cedar tree with horizontally spreading branches. Native to Lebanon and Turkey, such trees have a long life span and may reach 100 feet (30 meters) in height. Page 111.

Chamorro: of the native peoples of Guam and the Mariana Islands, in the western Pacific Ocean. Guam is the largest and southernmost of the Mariana Islands. The Mariana Islands extend north 1,565 miles (2,500 kilometers) from Guam almost to Japan. Page 17.

Charlemagne: Charlemagne Masséna Péralte (1885–1919), leader of a rebellion (named the *Cacos rebellion*) against the first United States occupation of Haiti (a country on an island of the West Indies, the chain of islands extending from the Florida peninsula to the coast of Venezuela). A *caco* is a peasant rebel from northern Haiti. Page 38.

cheechalker: a *tenderfoot,* an inexperienced person; someone who has recently arrived. From a Native North American language of the Alaskan coast. Page 56.

Chris Craft: an L. Ron Hubbard speedboat, the *Ulysses,* built by the Chris Craft Corporation, a manufacturer of powerboats. Page 146.

cinematographic: relating to, used in or connected with *cinematography,* the art, science and work of photography in making films. Page 191.

Citadelle Laferrière: a famous mountain fortress constructed on top of a 3,100-foot (1,000-meter) peak outside the city of Cap Haitien in Haiti. Page 38.

clipper: a term used in the names of some aircraft that fly over bodies of water, from a type of fast sailing ship first built in the mid-1800s. Page 58.

collecting lens: a lens that is thickest at its center and thinner toward its outer portions. This type of lens causes light passing through it to tend to come together at a point. Page 185.

College Park: a town near Washington, DC, established in 1745. The US Army Aviation School was established at the College Park Airfield in 1911 with aviation pioneer Wilbur Wright (1867–1912) as an instructor. The historic airport is the world's oldest in continuous operation. Page 38.

Columbia: a motion picture studio established in Hollywood, California, during the 1920s, becoming one of the largest US film companies. Page 158.

Columbia, California: a former California gold rush town founded in 1850 and now a well-preserved historic landmark and state historic park. The town is also the location of Saint Anne's Church, built in the early 1850s. Its bell, which was brought by sailing ship from the East Coast, was hung in the belfry in 1857. Page 194.

Columbus, Christopher: (1451–1506) Italian explorer, in Spanish service, who sailed across the Atlantic Ocean in search of a westward sea route to Asia and was responsible for the European discovery of America in 1492. (In Italian his name is Cristoforo Colombo and, in Spanish, Cristóbal Colón.) Page 171.

come what may: anything that; whatever. Page 218.

comm lag: short for *communication lag. Comm lag* means a delay; a delay in time; a delay in registering something, due to the inability of the person to get two things connected easily and rationally and to disconnect them at will. For instance, you tell the person how to start a car; he just can't register, it doesn't come across. Then much later it will suddenly and abruptly come to him and he will start the car. That's a communication lag. Page 223.

Conquistadores: Spanish conquerors of Mexico and Peru in the sixteenth century. Page 47.

coolie: an unskilled worker, especially formerly in China or India. Page 29.

Corfu: an island that is part of Greece; the northernmost of the *Ionian Islands,* a group of islands that lie off the northwestern coast of Greece and southwestern coast of Albania. Page 181.

Corozal: a town in north central Puerto Rico. Page 47.

Cousteau, Jacques-Yves: (1910–1997) French oceanographer, filmmaker and inventor who popularized the study of ocean environments through numerous books, films and television programs that described his undersea investigations. Page 89.

Creston, California: a rural community in central California, founded in the late 1800s. Page 193.

Crown Graphic: a Graflex press camera produced from the late 1940s until the 1970s. As with the other members of the Graflex family of cameras, the Crown Graphic produces superior-quality, medium-format photographs. *See also* **Graflex.** Page 66.

Cruikshank, George: (1792–1878) English illustrator born in London. He began his career with satirical political cartoons, depicting everything from great statesmen to common people, from church scenes to tavern brawls, including a famous series of drawings on the evils of drunkenness. As an illustrator, he worked closely with a number of authors, his work with Charles Dickens being particularly memorable. *See also* **Dickensian air.** Page 87.

cum: combined with, as in *"student-cum-assistant,"* a person who was a student combined with being an assistant. Page 198.

Curaçao: an island in the southern Caribbean Sea, lying off the coast of Venezuela. The island, an autonomous country within the Kingdom of the Netherlands, is a popular tourist destination. Page 157.

D

da Gama, Vasco: (1469?–1524) Portuguese explorer and navigator, the first European to reach India by the sea route. Page 3.

daylights, the living: a phrase used to emphasize the intensity or thoroughness of an action. Page 179.

day, of the: of the time period referred to or under consideration. Page 29.

Deardorff: a handmade view camera used by professionals for studio work, architecture and landscapes. The creation of American inventor Laben Deardorff (1862–1952), the large-format Deardorffs began production in the 1920s. *See also* **view camera.** Page 95.

dekalogy: a group of ten related volumes, from Greek *deka-,* ten, and *-logy,* a collection or group of writings. Page 151.

Dianetics: Dianetics is a forerunner and substudy of Scientology. Dianetics means "through the mind" or "through the soul" (from Greek *dia,* through, and *nous,* mind or soul). It is a system of coordinated axioms which resolve problems concerning human behavior and psychosomatic illnesses. It combines a workable technique and a thoroughly validated method for increasing sanity, by erasing unwanted sensations and unpleasant emotions. Page 17.

Dickensian air: a quality like that found in the works of Charles Dickens (1812–1870), prolific English novelist of the mid-nineteenth century whose books are noted for extravagant characters in the lower classes of England. Page 87.

dictum: a short statement that expresses a general truth or principle. Page 104.

diffusing screen: a device composed of material that lets light pass but spreads it out, making it less bright or intense. Page 185.

diggin's: an informal expression for *diggings,* a place where gold, precious stones or the like are removed by digging. Page 47.

Dominican Republic: a country in the West Indies, occupying part of the island of Hispaniola. Page 171.

downs: treeless, hilly areas with fairly smooth slopes usually covered with grass, particularly as found in southern England. Page 3.

drive a blade home: stab a sword into the body of a bull so that it pierces a vital organ, e.g., the heart. Page 141.

dryer: a cabinet with interior wires and clips for hanging developed film or prints while drying, used with or without a separate heat source, such as one blowing a gentle, filtered flow of warm air. Page 91.

E

Eagle Scout: a Boy Scout who has reached the highest level of attainment in various tests of skill and endurance. The Boy Scouts are a worldwide organization founded in England in 1908 that teaches boys to be self-reliant, resourceful and courageous. Page 12.

estuary: an inlet or arm of the sea; especially, the lower portion or wide mouth of a river, where the salty tide meets the freshwater current. Page 3.

Explorers Club: an organization, headquartered in New York and founded in 1904, devoted exclusively to promoting the science of exploration. To further this aim, it provides grants for those who wish to participate in field research projects and expeditions. It has provided logistical support for some of the twentieth century's most daring expeditions. L. Ron Hubbard was a lifetime member of the Explorers Club. Page 51.

Explorers Club flag: a flag awarded to active members of the Explorers Club who are in command of, or serving with, expeditions of legitimate scientific concern. The Explorers Club flag has been used by many famous persons in history who have belonged to the club, including L. Ron Hubbard. Page 51.

exposure: the total amount of light that reaches the film in a camera. Exposure has to be correct because if too much light enters the camera, the picture will be too bright. If there is not enough light, the picture will be too dark. Page 2.

F

f: as noted on the photographic test chart, *f* is an abbreviation for *f-number* or *f-stop,* a number that shows the width of the hole in a camera lens, through which light passes to expose the film. By rotating a ring around the camera lens, the size of the hole (also known as the *aperture* or *stop*) can be opened to allow more light to enter the camera or closed to reduce the amount of light. As the ring is turned, marks around the edge show the aperture settings, or f-stops. The higher the f-stop, the less light is allowed into the camera through the aperture. For example, the aperture is quite small at f16, more open at f8 and open even wider at f5.6. The letter *f* comes from *focal* or *focus.* Page 212.

film back(s): on some cameras, the rear panel of the camera, which includes the film. A film back of one camera is often interchangeable with another camera. One common use is to put a Polaroid back on another camera. Since the Polaroid back contains film that develops instantly, a shot can be taken of a given scene to determine beforehand the effects of flash lighting, etc. Page 161.

film sheet: photographic film prepared as sheets of various sizes for individual exposure when held in holders in a camera. Page 11.

film speed: *speed* means the sensitivity of a film to light. A fast film is very sensitive to light and needs little exposure. A slow film is not so sensitive to light and needs more exposure. Page 2.

fisherfolk: people who catch fish for a living. Page 51.

fisheye lens: a wide-angle lens that gives a very wide field of view, in which straight lines appear curved. Page 172.

floater: a person without a fixed place to live or regular employment; tramp. Page 60.

focus: the sharpness of the image in a photograph. The degree of sharpness is determined by (1) the distance between the camera lens and the subject and (2) the distance between the lens and the film inside the camera. Both factors can be adjusted by the photographer to get a sharp image. Page 2.

format, large-: a size of camera and film producing prints in the range (in inches) of 5 × 4, 10 × 8, etc. (in centimeters, roughly 13 × 10, 25 × 20), especially suitable for high-quality photographs, such as portraits, etc. Page 117.

format, medium-: a size of camera and film producing prints that are midway in size between large format and 35mm format, giving excellent quality photographs (though not as high quality as large-format cameras) and without having to use the large size cameras that produce large-format prints. Page 153.

format, 35mm: a size of camera and film developed in the early 1900s and still the most-used film size. The width of the film is 35 millimeters (about 1.4 inches), enabling very good quality photographs and smaller cameras that are easier to carry and use than larger cameras. Page 161.

forte: strong point; a particularly good quality or characteristic. Page 2.

Fossett's Circus, Sir Robert: one of the oldest of English circuses, founded in the 1800s by Robert Fossett (?–1874). The circus grew from several performing birds and a fortunetelling pony into a full circus. It has been carried on as a family operation by succeeding generations of Fossetts ever since. There are two Fossett Circuses, one in England and one in Ireland, both run by relatives of the original Fossett family. Page 104.

fulcrum and balance: a *fulcrum* is a stationary object on which a lever (a rigid bar) rests or is supported, leaving the two ends of the lever free. With the fulcrum in the middle of the lever, balance is possible if equal weights are on either end. But to achieve balance with different weights at either end, the heavier weight has to be closer to the fulcrum and the smaller weight further from the fulcrum on the other end of the lever. A description of visual balance paralleling the fulcrum balance is found in some works on composition. These point out that a painting or photograph can have a central area (fulcrum) and, on one side, small objects at a distance while, on the other side, larger ones positioned closer. Page 221.

full house, straight flush and two pairs: in the game of poker, a *full house* is a hand consisting of three cards of the same value and a set of two cards with a different value (for example, three kings and two queens); a *straight flush* (the highest-ranking hand of cards) is a hand in which all five cards form a continuous sequence of the same suit; a *two pair* has the lowest rank of the three, being literally two sets of two cards, each set having a different value. Page 56.

Funchal: the seaport capital of the *Madeira Islands,* a group of eight islands off the northwest coast of Africa, a part of Portugal. Page 142.

fuselage, leaning out to clear the: the fuselage is the body of the airplane not including the wings. The statement *"leaning out to clear the fuselage"* means leaning out over the edge of the open cockpit of the aircraft to avoid getting the fuselage in the picture. Page 38.

G

gaff: fish with a *gaff,* a large, strong hook on a pole, or a barbed spear, used to pull large fish out of the water. Page 59.

Gandolfi: the brand name of cameras produced by the British firm of Gandolfi & Sons, founded in the late 1800s and known for their traditional methods of manufacture. Page 151.

glass negative: also *glass-plate negative,* a sheet of glass coated with light-sensitive chemicals for use with special cameras. Glass negatives came into use in the mid-1800s, replacing the earlier paper negatives. The smooth glass negatives could produce sharper images than paper ones, because the details were no longer lost in the texture of the paper. Page 3.

glazer: a mechanical device used to produce a glossy surface on a print. This is achieved by placing a wet print face down on the heated, polished surface of the glazer. A glazed print produces denser blacks than prints not so glazed. Page 91.

Graflex: cameras designed and produced by the Folmer Graflex Corporation of Rochester, New York. The Graflex was the leading press camera, a portable camera for professional use, from the 1930s through the late 1950s. Page 1.

grain: in film, extremely tiny particles that, when exposed to light and developed, form the image. Sometimes these particles clump together, creating a spotted appearance in the final image.

To produce a very clear picture with no graininess, film must be prepared so that the particles are smaller than normal and are evenly distributed. Page 213.

Grand Canary (Island): one of the *Canary Islands,* a group of Spanish islands in the Atlantic Ocean, located southwest of Spain and about 60 miles (97 kilometers) off the northwest coast of Africa. Page 128.

Graphex: also *Speed Graphic Graphex,* a type of camera produced by Graflex. Known for its portability, the Graphex was a medium-format press camera. Page 131.

gunwale: the top edge of a ship's sides that forms a ledge around the whole ship above the deck. Page 164.

H

Hanukkah: an eight-day Jewish festival that occurs during December. Hanukkah is celebrated with the lighting of one of the lights of the menorah each day, to honor the rededication of the Temple in Jerusalem. This rededication occurred in 165 B.C., after a period during which the Temple had been taken over by a foreign ruler for the worship of Greek gods. *See also* **menorah.** Page 168.

heard tell: learned of or been informed about something. Page 3.

heart in the throat: characterized by anxious or fearful feelings, used in reference to the violent beating and apparent leaping of the heart due to a sudden startle or frightening situation. Page 51.

heels of, on the: closely following; just after. Page 47.

Hekhal: the ornate cabinet in a Jewish synagogue that contains the scriptures (Torah). When the scriptures are removed from the Hekhal, they are carried to the Theba (pulpit), located in the center of the synagogue. Standing in the Theba, the rabbi faces the Hekhal when reading from the scriptures. *See also* **Theba.** Page 168.

hilt, to the: to the furthest degree possible; completely, thoroughly. Page 181.

hinterland: an area far from big cities and towns. Page 1.

horn through the head, took a: received a thrust in the head from a bull's horn. Page 141.

Hunt, Sir John: (1910–1998) British mountaineer and explorer who led a British expedition that was the first to successfully reach the top of Mount Everest, the highest mountain (29,035 feet [8,850 meters]) in the world. Page 89.

Hydrographic Office: a section of the Department of the Navy charged with making hydrographic surveys and publishing charts and other information for naval and commercial vessels, information key to national defense. *Hydrographic* means of or relating to the scientific charting, description and analysis of the physical conditions, boundaries and flow of oceans, lakes, rivers, etc. Page 51.

I

ifil: a medium-sized, slow-growing evergreen tree whose wood is known for its hardness and durability. Page 19.

illusion, under no: understanding a situation correctly; not having an incorrect idea about something. Page 109.

inboard boat: a boat that has a motor located inside the hull, not fitted to the outside. Page 58.

infrared: a form of energy that can be used in motion detectors. A beam of infrared is sent out and when something moving cuts across the path of the beam, this interruption breaks a circuit and activates another mechanism. In the case of a camera, the mechanism activated is the shutter release, enabling the camera to photograph the image. *Infrared* literally means *below* (infra) *red* (light), meaning a lower energy than the energy of red light and not visible to the human eye. Page 118.

inscrutable: mysterious, unfathomable or not easily understood; incapable of being investigated or analyzed easily. Page 17.

J

Jaguar XK 150: a luxury sports car model produced by the famous race-car manufacturer Jaguar Cars Limited of London, England. The XK was a much-sought-after street model made between 1957 and 1961 and capable of speeds of over 130 miles (215 kilometers) per hour. Page 81.

Japanese puzzle box: a handcrafted wooden box engineered so that its sides can be moved, but only in a specific way and in a precise sequence, in order to trigger the locks and slide open the lid. The surfaces of these boxes are covered with intricate patterns of inlaid wood that serve to hide the mechanisms that lock the box. Page 115.

Journal of Scientology: a magazine for Scientologists that was published twice monthly from 1952 to 1955. The *Journal of Scientology* carried technical articles, information of broad interest to members, general news and the like. Page 68.

K

ketch: a two-masted sailing boat with sails set lengthwise (fore and aft) and with the mast closer to the front taller than the mast behind. Page 47.

Ketchikan: a seaport in southeastern Alaska, one of the chief ports on Alaska's Pacific coast. Ketchikan is a transportation and communications center. Page 51.

Klawock: a community in southeastern Alaska, situated on an island roughly 56 miles (90 kilometers) west of Ketchikan. Founded in the mid-1800s, Klawock is a fishing area with one of the only airports in the region. Page 58.

Koni Rapid Omega: a camera with a feature for measuring the distance to the subject being photographed, enabling the photographer to take sharp, focused pictures. Page 145.

L

Land, Professor: Edwin Herbert Land (1909–1991), an American inventor and scientist. He was founder, president and head of research of the *Polaroid Corporation,* an American camera and film manufacturer founded in the 1930s. He introduced the world's first instant camera and also developed the Polaroid Land Camera in 1947. Page 3.

Langley Day race: an air meet held around 6 May each year at College Park Airfield in Washington, DC, named in honor of aviation pioneer Samuel Langley who designed the first unmanned heavier-than-air craft able to sustain flight. Page 38.

La Quinta: a desert community located in Southern California. The town grew up around the famous La Quinta Resort, a golf resort established in the late 1920s. Page 188.

Las Palmas: a seaport in and capital of the Canary Islands, located on Grand Canary Island. *See also* **Grand Canary (Island).** Page 3.

last word, the: something regarded as the best or most advanced of its kind. Page 180.

late of: recently in the place mentioned. Page 37.

launch, motor: a large motorboat. Page 58.

Leica: a brand name for a line of cameras first produced at the Ernst Leitz optical firm in Wetzlar, Germany. The first Leica (named for *Leitz* and *camera*) was introduced to the public in 1924. The *Leica IIIb* was part of the *Leica III series,* cameras that had a feature for finding the range (distance to the subject), which improved focusing. Page 51.

Leica R4: one of a family of Leica cameras (the Leica R series) that included electronic features. *See also* **Leica.** Page 204.

lengths to which (one) went: the extent to which one went in trying to accomplish something. Page 83.

light test: a way of testing film to determine its performance relative to the amount of light in the scene. *See also* **test(ing) pattern.** Page 196.

Lincoln Memorial: a monument in Washington, DC, built in memory of Abraham Lincoln (1809–1865), sixteenth president of the United States (1861–1865). The building is 80 feet (24 meters) high, 189 feet (58 meters) long and 118 feet (36.2 meters) wide. It is constructed mainly of marble, granite and limestone and houses a 19-feet-tall (5.8 meters) statue of Lincoln seated in a chair and surrounded by a great hall. The monument is situated at the opposite end of the Reflecting Pool from the Washington Monument. Page 12.

Lindbergh: Charles Lindbergh (1902–1974), American aviator and engineer who made the first nonstop flight across the Atlantic, from New York to Paris (1927). His airplane was named *Spirit of St. Louis* (after the city of St. Louis, Missouri). Lindbergh's feat gained him immediate international fame and forwarded the American public's fascination with flying. Page 37.

Linhof: one of LRH's view cameras, particularly used for self-portraits and for fieldwork. The large film sheets of such cameras, such as 5 × 7 inches (roughly 12 × 18 centimeters), record images with a far greater wealth of detail than can be made with smaller-format films. *See also* **film sheet** and **view camera.** Page 1.

Linhof Technika: a Linhof camera produced since the 1930s and renowned as an exceptionally fine large-format *field camera,* the type of camera designed and built for both indoor and outdoor photography. One of the top cameras for precision and detail, the Technika models fold into a compact box for carrying. Page 96.

Lisbon estuary: the city of Lisbon, capital of Portugal, is located on the Tagus River, a 600-mile-long (966-kilometer) river that runs through Spain and Portugal to the Atlantic Ocean. As the river empties into the ocean, a broad estuary is formed. An *estuary* is an inlet or arm of the sea; especially, the lower portion or wide mouth of a river, where the salty tide meets the freshwater current. The Portuguese name of the river is *Tejo* and the Spanish name is *Tajo.* Page 3.

luminaries: persons who inspire or influence others. Page 38.

M

Madeira: the chief island of the *Madeira Islands,* a group of eight islands off the northwest coast of Africa, a part of Portugal. Page 142.

main, in the: in most cases; generally; usually. Page 145.

Mamiya RB67: a single-lens reflex camera first produced in the early 1970s by the Japanese company Mamiya, a firm that has manufactured high-quality cameras for professional use since the 1940s. The *RB,* for *revolving back,* incorporates a feature that allows the back of the camera to be quickly switched between portrait and landscape orientations. Page 160.

maneuver, on: during large-scale practice movements and exercises of troops, warships, aircraft, etc., under simulated combat conditions. Page 9.

manganese: a hard, brittle, grayish-white metallic element, used chiefly in steel to give it toughness. Page 47.

manufacture(s): something made or produced; product. Page 92.

Marianas: a group of islands in the western Pacific Ocean. Guam is the largest and southernmost of the Marianas, which extend north 1,565 miles (2,500 kilometers) from Guam almost to Japan. Page 17.

maritime museum, Portuguese: the maritime (relating to the sea) museum located in Lisbon, Museu de Marinha, founded in the mid-1800s and one of the premier maritime museums of Europe, with artifacts and models covering the nautical (relating to ships or sailors) history of Portugal. Page 3.

Martinique: an island in the West Indies (a group of islands in the Atlantic between North and South America). It was colonized by French settlers after 1635. Page 38.

Maspalomas: a town on the southern coast of Grand Canary Island. *See also* **Grand Canary (Island).** Page 131.

Mathieu, Matty: Hubert "Matty" Mathieu (1897–1954), American painter, sculptor, illustrator, lecturer and writer. Mathieu created a wide variety of art and was well known for producing illustrations for magazines and newspapers, as well as for his portraiture. Page 220.

Mecablitz: a model of electronic flash made by *Metz,* a German manufacturer of consumer electronics products. This type of flash, which emits a brief flash of light while a picture is being taken, replaced the *flashbulb,* a disposable, single-use device. Page 139.

menorah: a Hebrew word meaning candlestick. The *menorah* is a holy lamp with eight lights or eight candles (with a ninth used to light the others), used in the Jewish festival of Hanukkah. On the first night of Hanukkah, one flame is lighted. One more flame is added every night until all eight are lighted on the last night of the festival. *See also* **Hanukkah.** Page 168.

merit badge: an insignia granted by the Boy Scouts, worn especially on a uniform to indicate special achievement. Page 9.

Merizo: a village on the southern tip of the island of Guam. Page 20.

Metz: the name of the German manufacturer of consumer electronics products, such as electronic flash equipment, as noted on the photographic test chart. *See also* **Mecablitz.** Page 212.

microammeter: an instrument for measuring electric current in *microamperes,* units of one-millionth of an ampere. *Micro-* means one-millionth and *ampere* is the standard unit for measuring the rate of flow of an electric current, that is, how much electricity is flowing per unit of time (per second). Page 185.

Micro-Press: a press camera first produced in the 1940s by the British optical company Micro Precision Products. As with similar press cameras, the Micro-Press was designed to collapse into a strong, compact box for carrying. Page 82.

millrace: a strong current of water flowing in a narrow channel. Literally, a *millrace* is the current of water that drives a mill wheel. The water of the millrace falls against the paddles attached to the mill wheel, pushing the mill wheel around and around. This, in turn, drives machinery, such as large stone wheels used for grinding grain to make flour. Page 51.

mine: a device containing a charge of explosive in a watertight casing, floating on or moored beneath the surface of the water for the purpose of blowing up an enemy ship that strikes it or passes close by it. Page 57.

Minolta: the brand name of cameras and camera accessories produced by a Japanese manufacturer, founded in the late 1920s. One of their most innovative products was the Minolta CLE (for *Compact Leica Electronic*), a precision camera that incorporated a Leitz lens from the famed Leica factory. *See also* **Leica.** Page 191.

Minox: a subminiature camera first produced in the mid-1930s, made by the Minox Company, which also produces optical equipment, such as binoculars. Page 191.

Modern Photography: a monthly magazine that was published during the 1900s, with articles and advertising on cameras and photographic equipment. Page 203.

moment: special importance or significance. Page 85.

mother lode country: the region in eastern and northeastern California in the western slopes of the Sierra Nevada (a mountain range in eastern California). This region contains a *mother lode,* a term associated with the mining of gold and referring to the main deposits or layers of rich gold. The discovery of gold in this region led to the California gold rush of 1849. (A *gold rush* is a large-scale movement of people to a region where gold has been discovered.) Page 194.

motor torpedo boat (MTB): also called *PT (patrol torpedo) boat,* a small, highly maneuverable naval vessel, used to torpedo enemy shipments. Page 57.

N

Nanking Road: also *Nanjing Road,* a famous street in Shanghai, China, and the city's principal shopping district. Page 29.

Nan-k'ou Pass: an opening through the Nan-k'ou mountain range in China about 50 miles (80 kilometers) north of Beijing (formerly Peking). The pass is the site of a fortified section of China's Great Wall, well known as the location of battles against invading tribes. A railway, linking Beijing to areas in the north, runs through the pass and through a gateway in the Great Wall itself. Page 31.

Nantes International Salon Exhibition: an international photography exhibit held in Nantes, a city in western France. The city is home to one of France's premier museums of fine arts, the Musée des Beaux-Arts, which has one of the most important and varied collections of paintings in the country. Page 109.

National Museum: the United States National Museum, located in Washington, DC, which includes major collections of American history and technology, and natural history. The National Museum is administered by the *Smithsonian Institution,* a group of scientific and cultural institutes created in 1846 from a grant given by British scientist James Smithson. Page 12.

naturalist: a person who studies nature, especially by direct observation of animals and plants. Page 14.

Nikon: the brand name of cameras produced by the Nikon Corporation of Japan, founded in 1917 as a major optical manufacturing concern. A 35mm, single-lens reflex camera first produced in the late 1950s, the Nikon F series immediately established itself as one of the most advanced cameras of its day and has consistently ranked as a top professional camera. Page 203.

nipa: a type of palm tree that grows in tropical parts of Asia and Australia, having large, feathery leaves that are woven together and used for roofing, baskets, mats and other such items. Page 27.

Norman castle: a castle built by the Normans, people from the region in northwestern France called *Normandy.* In 1066, William, Duke of Normandy, invaded England and became the first of the Norman kings to rule England. His descendents ruled until 1485. Page 85.

O

Oak Knoll Naval Hospital: a naval hospital located in Oakland, California, USA, where LRH spent time recovering from injuries sustained during World War II (1939–1945) and researching the effect of the mind on the physical recovery of patients. Page 194.

Oakland: a seaport in western California, on San Francisco Bay, opposite the city of San Francisco. Page 194.

Olympus: the brand name of a Japanese company established in 1919 as a manufacturer of optical goods. The first Olympus cameras were produced in the mid-1930s. The designation "OM" (originally just "M" for mechanical) covered a camera system that introduced a compact format of cameras and lenses. Page 202.

100: *Polaroid Land Automatic 100,* a camera developed by the Polaroid Corporation in 1963. The Polaroid 100 automatically measured the light level, exposed the film the correct length of time and then immediately produced a print. The camera used either color or black and white film. Also called *Automatic 100*. Page 100.

Oporto: the second-largest city in Portugal and an Atlantic port, located along the Douro River, 175 miles (280 kilometers) north of Lisbon. Page 184.

optical wedge: a wedge-shaped filter that transmits light in gradually decreasing amounts from one end of the wedge to the other. Optical wedges are used as exposure control devices to reduce the intensity of light gradually or in steps. Page 185.

order, in: being suitable to the occasion; fitting; appropriate. Page 175.

P

pace with, in: maintaining the same speed of movement; advancing at an equal rate; keeping up with. Page 219.

Panhandle: part of the state of Alaska that extends along the Pacific coast, south from the main part of the state. A *panhandle* is a narrow section of land shaped like the handle of a cooking pan, that extends away from the body of the state it belongs to. Page 51.

panorama(s): a photograph that includes a wide view of a scene or group of people made by joining separate photographs or by means of a special camera that automatically turns so that adjacent areas of the film are exposed consecutively. Page 20.

Parthenon: a temple to Athena built in Athens, Greece, in the fifth century B.C. Located on the Acropolis—the elevated, fortified section of the city—the Parthenon is one of the best examples of ancient Greek architecture. Page 72.

pastoral: a photograph that presents a pleasant scene of the countryside or rural life. Page 109.

Pentax: a Japanese camera, product of the Asahi Optical Company (founded in 1919). Pentax ES cameras were one of the first 35mm cameras to include a fully electronic shutter system. Page 145.

photoelectric cell: a device sensitive to varying levels of light, that is used to generate or control an electric current, for example, in exposure meters. Page 185.

photoflood: a very bright floodlight (a light that gives a beam of intense illumination) used in photography. Photofloods have the appearance of ordinary household bulbs but are much brighter. They are usually used with reflectors (curved, shiny metallic plates) and are capable of providing continuous intense light for several hours. Page 181.

photojournalist: a person involved in *photojournalism,* the communicating of news by photographs. Page 38.

Piti: a town and port in southwestern Guam (a territory of the United States) in the northwest Pacific Ocean. Page 23.

Plaza de Toros: a Spanish term meaning a *bullring,* an arena where bullfights are held. Page 136.

plying: running or traveling regularly over a fixed course or between certain places, said of ships and other vehicles. Page 29.

point-and-shoot: a term used to describe cameras that require no adjustment by the user before taking a photograph because the camera controls the focus and various other settings automatically. Page 11.

Polaroid back: the rear panel of a Polaroid camera, including the film. A Polaroid back is often interchangeable with another camera. Since the Polaroid back contains film that develops instantly, a shot can be taken of a given scene to determine beforehand the effects of flash lighting, etc. Page 99.

Polaroid Land Automatic 100: a camera developed by the Polaroid Corporation in 1963. The Polaroid 100 automatically measured the light level, exposed the film the correct length of time and then immediately produced a print. The camera used either color or black and white film. Also called *Automatic 100* or *100.* Page 99.

Polaroid Land Camera: a camera invented by Edwin Herbert Land (1909–1991), an American inventor, scientist and business executive, founder of the American Polaroid Corporation in the 1930s. The Polaroid Land Camera was the first practical instant camera. Developed in the late 1940s, the camera produced instant prints on special film in less than a minute of the shot's being taken. Page 3.

Pontiac Bonneville: a luxury car built by automobile manufacturer General Motors. The Bonneville models included some of the longest US cars ever built, with large, powerful engines and many other features that ranked it as one of the superior models of American cars. Page 87.

Popular Photography: an American monthly magazine with information on photographic techniques and equipment, published since the late 1930s. Page 203.

Port Huron: a city and port at the southern tip of Lake Huron in southeastern Michigan, a state in the north central United States. Page 37.

Port Royal: a historic harbor town on the southern coast of Jamaica, an island in the West Indies, and a base of operations for pirates until the late seventeenth century, when the existing town was destroyed by an earthquake. The partly submerged ruins remain at the entrance to the present-day harbor. Page 157.

port(s) of call: a harbor town or city where ships can visit during the course of a voyage. Page 9.

precipitous: proceeding rapidly or with great haste. Page 9.

pro: short for *professional,* a person showing an extremely high degree of skill or competence in a specific field; expert. Hence, *pro-line,* professional-line, designating a set (line) of equipment designed for use by professionals. Page 100.

Prohibition: a period in the United States (1920–1933) in which the manufacture, transportation and sale of alcoholic liquors for beverage purposes were forbidden by federal law. Many people ignored the national ban. Page 115.

protectorship: the state of being protected or defended, used with reference to the status of Puerto Rico, an island in the Caribbean Sea associated with the United States and having self-government in local matters. Page 1.

Puget Sound: a long, narrow bay of the Pacific Ocean on the coast of Washington, a state in the northwestern United States. Page 6.

Purification Rundown: a program to purify and clean out of one's system the restimulative drug or chemical residues that could act to prevent gains from Dianetics and Scientology processing. Page 191.

R

rafters, to the: all the way up to the very top (*rafters* are literally the beams that support a roof). Page 107.

range shift disc: a device for varying the brightness range of the SEI meter. Page 185.

Reflecting Pool: the long, narrow pool stretching between the Washington Monument and the Lincoln Memorial in Washington, DC. Page 12.

Reflex-Korelle: a German camera produced between the mid-1930s and the early 1950s. The Korelle was a single-lens reflex camera, one with an internal mirror that reflects the actual image from the lens into the viewfinder so that the photographer can check the composition and focus exactly. The mirror is hinged; at the moment the photographer snaps the picture, a spring automatically pulls the mirror out of the path between lens and film, allowing the image to be recorded on the film. Because of this system, the image recorded on the film is almost exactly what the photographer sees in the viewfinder. Page 65.

rheostat: a device that operates in an electric circuit to gradually increase or decrease the flow of current, as with lights that can be varied in brightness. Page 184.

ringmaster: somebody who presides over a circus show from a ring (a circular stage or piece of ground for performances), announcing and commenting on the events. Page 3.

Rock Creek Park: a large park in Washington, DC, running along Rock Creek, containing extensive recreational facilities and covering 1,800 acres of natural woodlands. Page 37.

Rolleicord: a camera made by Franke & Heidecke, the German manufacturer of Rolleiflex cameras. With controls somewhat simpler than those for the Rolleiflex, Rolleicords were known for producing high-quality, medium-format photographs and could also be adapted for 35mm. *See also* **format, medium-** and **format, 35mm.** Page 65.

Rolleiflex: a camera manufactured by a German company, Franke & Heidecke. The Rolleiflex (or Rollei) was extremely popular with both amateur and professional photographers due to its precision, durability and compact size. Page 3.

Rollei 35: a miniature 35mm camera first produced in Germany in the late 1960s. Starting with its original compact design, Rollei 35s have included numerous inventive features, such as a lens that collapsed into the body, making it one of the most consistently popular cameras of its size. Page 146.

roustabout: a deckhand or waterfront laborer. Page 51.

ruby bulb district: a humorous variation of *red-light district,* an area with many houses of prostitution, which formerly displayed a red light in a doorway or window. Page 59.

Ryan, Claude: Tubal Claude Ryan (1898–1982), American aviator and aircraft manufacturer. Ryan began flying in 1917 and, through the years, was responsible for notable advances in the design and manufacture of airplanes, such as American aviator Charles Lindbergh's plane *Spirit of St. Louis* and the Ryan ST, which was used by the US Army as a basic training plane. (*ST* stands for *Sport Trainer.*) *See also* **Lindbergh.** Page 38.

S

Saint Hill: the name of the manor (large house and its land) purchased by L. Ron Hubbard in 1959, located in East Grinstead, Sussex, England. Saint Hill Manor served as LRH's home and was where he carried out much of his research from 1959 to 1966. Page 1.

sample pick: a type of lightweight, hand-held pick used by prospectors and miners in taking samples, often having a square head on one end for hammering into surfaces and a pointed tip on the other end for breaking up ore. Taking samples involves striking off bits of rock along a rock face, collecting the bits and then having them analyzed to determine their mineral content. Page 47.

San Antonio: a town on the west coast of the island of Guam. Page 27.

sanctuary: the area around the altar in a Christian church, which is the holiest part of the church. Page 171.

Santo Domingo: capital and largest city of the Dominican Republic, a country founded by Spain in the 1500s and occupying the eastern part of the island of Hispaniola in the Caribbean Sea. Page 171.

Sargasso Sea: an irregular oval-shaped area of the western North Atlantic Ocean, northeast of the Caribbean, whose boundaries are defined by four ocean currents. Inside these currents, the waters of the Sargasso are calmer, warmer and more salty than the waters of the flowing currents. The name comes from the brown seaweed that floats in massive clumps on the still surface of the water. Page 43.

scat, faster than: a variation of the phrase *quicker than scat,* meaning extremely quickly. *Scat* is used here as an intensification. Page 3.

scenic: a photograph featuring scenery rather than figures and stressing the beauties of nature. Page 101.

schooner: a sailing ship with sails set lengthwise (fore and aft) and having from two to as many as seven masts. Page 29.

Scientology: Scientology is the study and handling of the spirit in relationship to itself, universes and other life. The term Scientology is taken from the Latin *scio,* which means "knowing in the fullest sense of the word," and the Greek word *logos,* meaning "study of." In itself the word means literally "knowing how to know." Page 17.

scratch, from: right from the beginning. A *scratch* is a line or mark drawn as an indication of a starting point in some sporting contest. Page 2.

Sears: a reference to Sears, Roebuck and Company, an American general-merchandise business composed of a chain of retail stores and one of the world's largest mail-order houses, founded in 1893. Page 56.

SEI: a light meter used in photography to measure the amount of light in a scene, from the name *Salford Electrical Instruments,* the original manufacturers. Page 184.

self-timer: a mechanism on a camera that can be set to delay the opening of the shutter until a specified time has elapsed, usually 2, 5 or 10 seconds. This delay allows any camera vibration to die down before the shutter opens, thus producing a sharper photograph. Page 101.

Shackleton, Ernest: (1874–1922) British explorer of Antarctica who led three expeditions to the Antarctic. One of these expeditions, in 1902, came within 111 miles (179 kilometers) of reaching the South Pole, the closest anyone had ever come at the time. Page 171.

shake things up: surprise people and make them look at things or think about things in a different way. Page 126.

shoal(s): a sandbar or piece of rising ground forming a shallow place in water that is a danger to ships. Page 164.

shutter: in a camera, a mechanical device that controls how long the film is exposed to light, as by opening and closing to allow light to come through the lens and onto the film. The speed with which a shutter opens and closes can range from a small fraction of a second (1/1000th of a second or less) to minutes or even hours and influences the appearance of the photograph. Page 2.

Sinar: a Swiss camera company founded in the late 1940s, manufacturers of high-precision, medium- and large-format view cameras. Sinar cameras are particularly known for interchangeability of parts and for having a wide assortment of accessories. Page 210.

single-lens reflex: a camera with an internal mirror that reflects the actual image from the lens into the viewfinder so that the photographer can check the composition and focus exactly. The mirror is hinged; at the moment the photographer snaps the picture, a spring automatically pulls the mirror out of the path between lens and film, allowing the image to be recorded on the film. Because of this system, the image recorded on the film is almost exactly what the photographer sees in the viewfinder. Page 65.

Sir Robert Fossett's Circus: one of the oldest of English circuses, founded in the 1800s by Robert Fossett (?–1874). The circus grew from several performing birds and a fortunetelling pony into a full circus. It has been carried on as a family operation by succeeding generations of Fossetts ever since. There are two Fossett Circuses, one in England and one in Ireland, both run by relatives of the original Fossett family. Page 104.

sluicing chute: also called a *sluice,* in mining, a long, sloping trough or the like, with grooves on the bottom, into which water is directed to separate gold from gravel or sand. Page 49.

Smith, Eugene: William Eugene Smith (1918–1978), American photojournalist best known for his work in creating photographs that communicate his moral concern for others. During World War II he served as a combat photographer in the Pacific. Page 79.

spawn: (of fish) produce or deposit eggs, sperm or young. Page 59.

speed, film: *speed* means the sensitivity of a film to light. A fast film is very sensitive to light and needs little exposure. A slow film is not so sensitive to light and needs more exposure. Page 2.

spill(s): a throw, as from a horse; a fall or tumble. Page 3.

stereo-optic images: images that show three-dimensional views. Page 51.

Stetson: a type of felt hat with a broad brim and a high crown, particularly popular in the western US. Named after John B. Stetson (1830–1906), who originated it in the mid-1800s. Page 37.

Stimson, Henry: Henry Lewis Stimson (1867–1950), influential US statesman who served under four United States presidents between 1911 and 1945. Stimson was Secretary of State from 1929 to 1933. Page 37.

stock shot: a photograph (as of an historical event or geographical area) from a library or store of shots kept for future use. Page 9.

stop scale: a scale showing *f-stops,* also called *f-numbers,* which designate the width of the hole in a camera lens that light passes through to expose the film. *See also* **f.** Page 185.

straits: a narrow body of water that joins two larger bodies of water. Page 55.

string-set shutter: a shutter mechanism on a Kodak box camera. It consisted of a piece of string connecting a brass knob on top of the camera and the shutter mechanism inside. When one pulled on the knob, the string cocked the shutter in preparation for shooting. Page 9.

strobe(s): also *strobe light,* a lamp capable of producing extremely short, brilliant bursts of light, used with a camera and synchronized with it (made to work at the same time or the same rate as). Page 168.

surfeits: supplies with anything to excess, so as to weary, disgust or nauseate. Page 141.

Sussex: a former county of southeastern England, now divided into two counties, East Sussex and West Sussex. Saint Hill is located in East Grinstead, West Sussex. Page 87.

switchman: a railroad worker who uses levers to control *switches,* track structures on a railroad for diverting moving trains from one track to another, commonly consisting of pairs of movable rails. Page 87.

T

telephoto lens: a type of lens that can function like a telescope, magnifying and bringing into focus a subject in the distance. Page 89.

tenderfoot: an inexperienced person. Page 56.

Tercer Hombre, El: Spanish for *The Third Man,* used as a name for a matador (the principal bullfighter in a bullfight, whose specialty is killing the bull with a sword thrust at the end of a fight). Page 141.

test(ing) pattern: an arrangement of progressively darker shades from white to black that is printed out on a board, card or the like and then shot with a particular type of film in a camera. A testing (or test) pattern is used to determine film performance relative to the amount of light in the scene. Page 213.

Theba: the pulpit in a Jewish synagogue, located in the center of the building. When the scriptures (Torah) are removed from the Hekhal, they are carried to the Theba. Standing in the Theba, the rabbi faces the Hekhal when reading from the scriptures. *See also* **Hekhal.** Page 168.

The Sportsman Pilot: a monthly American aviation magazine published from around 1930 until 1943. It contained writings on a wide range of subjects, including coverage of aerial sporting events, commentary on current aviation issues, technical articles on flying as well as other articles on topics of general interest. Page 37.

35mm: (of a camera) designed for or able to be used with film measuring 35 millimeters (approximately 1.4 inches) in width. Such cameras and film have been popular for years due to their compactness and economy. (A *millimeter* is a unit of length equal to one-thousandth of a meter, or .039 inch.) Page 136.

3000 film: a type of black and white film produced by the Polaroid Corporation and used for taking instant photos. The number indicates a fast *film speed,* the sensitivity of a film to light. *See also* **film speed.** Page 100.

timber wolf: the name in North America for the gray wolf (also simply *wolf*), the large, gray member of the wild dog family found especially in forested regions of northern Europe, Asia and North America. The wolf hunts in packs and is noted for its fierceness. Page 198.

Tlingit: a Native North American people of the coastal regions of southern Alaska and northern British Columbia, Canada. Page 60.

token, by the same: in like manner; similarly. Page 17.

toll, take a: have an adverse effect, especially so as to cause damage or suffering. Page 58.

Tongass Narrows: a narrow body of water in southeastern Alaska. The port of Ketchikan is situated on the Tongass Narrows. Page 57.

tong-paddle: a tool for seizing, holding or lifting something, having two arms with flat, circular pieces like small paddles at the ends. At the other end, near the handle, the arms are hinged so they can be pressed together in a pinching movement around the item to be lifted. A tong-paddle is used in a darkroom for lifting photographic prints from trays of photographic chemicals. Page 17.

topographer: a person trained in *topography,* the detailed mapping or charting of the features of an area on a map. Page 51.

tortuous: not direct; full of twists, turns or bends. Page 47.

Tower of Belém: a white tower built in the early 1500s, located at the mouth of the Tagus River. *See also* **Lisbon estuary**. Page 145.

trade secret: literally, a secret method or technique used to advantage in a trade, business or profession. Used figuratively to describe an inventive solution used in taking a photograph. Page 168.

trammeling: a tangling up or a hindering so that something is prevented from moving freely. Page 3.

treat, quite a: something highly enjoyable. Page 43.

Trinidad: an island country off the coast of South America, the most southerly of the West Indies. It consists of the two islands, Trinidad and Tobago, discovered by Christopher Columbus in 1498. Page 158.

Tumon: a beach area, now a resort, on the west coast of the island of Guam. Page 23.

turns, by: one after another; in rotation or succession; alternately. Page 68.

two-G drop: a downward plunge of an aircraft that is forceful enough to produce the effect of two Gs. A *G* is a unit of force equal to the force exerted on a body by gravity when it undergoes rapid acceleration (such as when an aircraft drops suddenly). Thus *two Gs* would be twice the amount of force or stress that the body feels under normal gravity. Page 38.

U

uncharted: not recorded or plotted on a *chart,* a map showing a portion of water along with the outline of the coasts, position of rocks, etc., intended especially for use by navigators. Page 3.

Underwood & Underwood: a former photographic firm, started in 1882 by brothers Elmer and Bert E. Underwood. Traveling throughout the world taking photographs of royalty, famous personalities and major news events, Elmer is credited by many as having introduced the first news pictures. By 1901 the firm was producing twenty-five thousand photos a day and supplying pictures from all over the world to newspapers and other publications. It continued in business into the late 1900s. Page 31.

Universal: a major Hollywood motion picture production company founded in 1912. Its film studios are among the largest in the world and are located near Los Angeles, California, in Universal City, a town built by the company. Page 158.

V

veldt: in southern and eastern Africa, open grassy country with few bushes and almost no trees. Page 89.

view camera: a camera having two main sections that can move back and forth on a track. The front section of the camera holds the lens and the back section holds the film. Fitted between these two sections is a *bellows,* flexible accordion-like leather sides that keep light out and which can be closed up and expanded, allowing the front and back sections to be moved toward and away from each other. These sections can also be shifted, tilted or raised separately, allowing for great variation in focus. With the special, precise viewing system used in such cameras, the photographer has the ability to achieve great accuracy in focusing the image before taking the picture. View cameras use film that is larger than the film used in nonprofessional cameras, allowing for much greater detail in photographs. Page 121.

vis-à-vis: in relation to. Page 79.

Voigtländer: the brand name of cameras produced by Voigtländer, a company formed in Vienna, Austria, in the mid-1700s to produce lenses and optical equipment. The company began manufacturing cameras in the mid-1800s and is known for its consistently high-quality products. Page 95.

W

W: an abbreviation for *watt,* a unit of electrical power. A *watt* is a measurement of the rate of flow of energy; that is, how much electrical energy is flowing per unit of time. Page 181.

Wang Po: an earlier spelling of *Huang-p'u,* a river in eastern China. The Huang-p'u serves as the harbor of Shanghai, one of the largest ports in the world, linking the city to the East China Sea. Page 31.

Washington Monument: the tall, white-marble, four-sided stone pillar tapering toward its pyramidal top, located in Washington, DC, that honors George Washington (1732–1799), the first president of the United States (1789–1797). It is 555 feet (169 meters) in height and is one of the tallest stonework structures in the world. It is situated at the opposite end of the Reflecting Pool from the Lincoln Memorial. Page 12.

weather: disagreeable atmospheric conditions, as in low clouds, storms or the like. Page 58.

Weir Wood Reservoir: a 1.5-mile-long (2.4-kilometer) lake located in southern England near East Grinstead. Constructed in the mid-1900s, Weir Wood Reservoir is partly a wildlife preserve and is also used for such activities as fishing and sailing. Page 103.

went off: was carried out or conducted in a particular manner. Page 141.

went so far as: dealt with something to a surprising extent or limit. Page 186.

whithers: places a person goes to. The article "West Indies Whys and Whithers" dealt with flying in the West Indies. Page 38.

INDEX

A

abandoned mine shaft, Puerto Rico

photograph, 46

Acropolis, Athens

photograph, 74–75

action shooting, 141

Adams, Ansel

SEI (Salford Electrical Instruments), use of, 184

Advance! **magazine**

Curaçao photo shoot, 158

aerial photography

camera, 36

Citadelle Laferrière, 38

The Sportsman Pilot, 37

Alaska

en route to

photograph, 55

photographs, 51–61

voyage, recharting coastline, 1

Albania from the shores of Corfu

photograph, 181

Apollo, 145

flying bridge

photograph, 144

photographic team, 158

sunset at Agadir, Morocco

photograph, 147

art

"authorities" and, 127

contribution and, 125

criticism and

types of, 126

definition, 124

divided opinion about a work, 126

most uncodified and least organized field, 127

originality and, 126

two-way communication and, 125

Athens

Acropolis, 65, 72

"authorities"

art and, 127

"Autumn Sky," southern England

photograph, 109

B

Battlefield Earth

New York Times bestseller, 194

beech grove, southern England

photograph, 84

beehive safelights, 91

billibutugun, 22

blue flash, 100

Bridge, Queen Juliana, Curaçao, 172–173

British Colour Council, 85

Britton, Jimmy

owner of KGBU radio station, 57

Bubba the Bull, Northern California

photograph, 199

bullfight

photographs, 141

C

Camera Room

LRH collection of camera and
photographic equipment, 206

cameras

aerial photography, 37

Canon, 72, 207

Deardorff, 95, 115, 210

self-portraits, 117

Gandolfi, 210, 222

5 × 4 view portrait camera, 151

Graflex, 1, 3, 38, 39, 47, 65, 208

Crown Graphic, 66–67, 209

single film sheet, 38

Speed Graphic, 209

Graphex, 130, 132

Kodak Brownie Jr., 8–11, 210

Koni Rapid Omega, 145, 156, 160–161,
209

Land Camera, 100

Leica, 204

Minolta CLE, 191, 193, 208

Minox, 191, 192, 208

R4, 204

IIIb, 51, 53

Linhof, 1, 3, 94, 121, 208

4 × 5, 121

5 × 7, 121

self-portraits, 117

Technika, 97

LRH collection of cameras, 206

Mamiya

C33, 153, 209

RB67, 160, 208

Micro-Press, 82, 209

Nikon, 208

F system, Nikon F3AF, 203

Nikonos, 135, 208

Olympus, 207

OM system
"Old Workhorse," 202

Pentax, 145, 161

    Auto 110, 209

    ES, 160, 172, 209

    6 × 7, 209

Polaroid, 207

    Land Automatic 100, 98–102

    Land Camera, 3, 100

Reflex-Korelle, 65

Rolleicord, 65, 101

Rollei (Rolleiflex), 3, 89, 104, 164, 209

    Rollei 35, 146, 209

    self-portraits, 117

Sinar F, 210

Sinar P, 210

35mm systems, 194, 202

Voigtländer, 95, 96, 163, 207, 210

    Bessamatic, 145

    camera system, 136

    Ultramatic, 145

camera stable data

    checklist, 223

    know them cold, 219

Camp Parsons, Washington

    photograph, 14–15

Canary Island historical sites

    photographs using Graphex and Nikonos, 131–135

Canon, 72, 207

Capitol Building, Washington, DC

    photograph, 12

Caribbean Motion Picture Expedition, 1, 43

Cartier-Bresson, Henri, 192

"cathedral lighting effect" off Las Palmas, Grand Canary Island

    photograph, 147

Cedar of Lebanon, Saint Hill, England

    photograph, 110

Chamorro culture, 20

checklist

    camera stable data, 223

China

    candid of life in

        photograph, 29

    photographs, 28–33

    Wang Po River, Shanghai

        photograph, 30

China's Great Wall

    photographs, 31, 32–33

circus

    Sir Robert Fossett's, 104–107

        elephant, 106

        Elephant Man, 104

        lion, 106

Citadelle Laferrière, Haiti

    photograph, 38

College Park, 38

color

    reproduction, tests to determine best, 213

    temperature, *see* **color temperature**

color compensation filter, 181

color temperature, 180

    color rendition and, 179

    definition, 179

filters and, 179

measurement of, 181

scale, 181

understanding basics of, 180

Columbus, Christopher

monuments photo shoot, 171

communication

art and quality of, 217

photography and, 217

composition

definition, 221

false data in field of composition, 221

fundamentals, 218

Matty Mathieu and abstract theory, 220

notes on, 221

constructive criticism

definition, 126

contribution

art and, 125

criticism and, 126

definition, 125

true art elicits, 125

Cousteau, Jacques-Yves

Rollei camera, 89

Creston, California, pastures

photographs, 200–201

Criterion 4000 telescope, 210

criticism

contribution and, 126

two types, 126

Crown Graphic, 66

Cruikshank, George, 87

Curaçao

home port of *Freewinds,* 172

newspaper articles on LRH, 158

Photo Shoot Organization, 157

Queen Juliana Bridge, 172

D
_____

dahlias, southern England

photograph, 86

darkroom

standard developing and printing line, 91

Deardorff, 210

an "old reliable" camera, 115

definitions

art, 124

color temperature, 179

composition, 221

constructive criticism, 126

contribution, 125

photography, 1

Doris Hamlin

photographs, 42–45

double rainbow over harbor entrance to Kontokali, Corfu, Greece

photograph, 224

E
_____

Earls Court Road, London

photograph, 69

East Grinstead, England

equestrian

photograph, 111

Jaguar XK 150 "camera car"

photograph, 80–81

photograph, 84

El Tercer Hombre, 141

equipment

collection of, 206

exhibition

selections for 9th Nantes International
Salon Exhibition, 109

**Experimental Aircraft, San Diego,
California**

photograph, 34–35

Explorers Club

Alaska, 51

Santo Domingo, Dominican
Republic, 171

F

field photography

challenge, 47

film

color temperature and, 179

combined tests of equipment and
film, 213

contrast, tests, 213

geographic location, color of light
and, 147

grain particles, test to analyze, 213

negative

lighting conditions and, 180

sheet, 11, 38, 40, 117

speed, 2

transparency (slide) film, 180

filters

arsenal of, 182

color compensation filter, 181

three categories, 179

flamenco dancers

photographs, 139

flash

blue flash, 100

guns, 207

Mecablitz, 139

system, 207

**fox-hunting dogs, East Grinstead,
England**

photograph, 70–71

fox hunt in Sussex, shot with a Rolleiflex

photograph, 112–113

framing

fundamentals, 218

Funchal, island of Madeira

photograph, 142–143

G

gadget bag

itemized contents, 196

Gandolfi, 151, 210, 222

George Washington University, 1

Gibraltar, overlooking

photograph, 135

Graflex, 1, 3, 38, 39, 47, 65, 208

aerial photography, 38

Crown Graphic, 66–67, 209

Speed Graphic, 209

Grand Canary Island

eastern shores

photograph, 134

Graphex, 130, 132

Great Wall of China, 31, 37

series, 29

Greece

photographs, 72

Guam

photographs, 16–27

H

Helena, Montana

boyhood home, 9

Hubbard, Harry Ross

portfolio, 9

Hubbard Method, The

printing procedure, 186

Hunt, Sir John

Rollei camera, 89

I

illustrations

color temperature scale, 181

literal, 125

SEI meter, 185

stereo photography, 52–53

innovation

art and, 126

instruction

in photography, 217–225

LRH instructional critiques, 218

J

Jaguar XK 150 "camera car," 81, 87

K

Kensington, London, England

photograph, 62–63

Ketchikan, Alaska, landfall in

photograph, 51

Kodak Brownie Jr., 8–11, 210

Kodak Instamatic

simplest of cameras, 217

Kodak Library of Creative Photography
series

LRH exercise to sharpen skills, 198

Kodak research laboratories

tropical film conditions

discussion, 43

Koni Rapid Omega, 145, 160–161, 209

photograph, 156

L

Langley Day race, 38

latter years, 191–204

    Creston, California, ranch

        carpenter, first camera, 198

        photographs, 199–201

Leica

    great-grandfather of all 35mm

        cameras, 204

    Minolta CLE, 191, 193, 208

    Minox, 191, 192, 208

    R4, 204

    IIIb, 51, 53

lens

    fisheye, 172

    performance and clarity, tests to

        eliminate variables, 213

    Stereoly lens, 51

    telephoto lens, 89, 204

    twin-lens, 89, 153, 164

    200mm (long range) lens, 141

lighthouse

    Maspalomas, Grand Canary Island

        photograph, 131

lighting

    film and color of light in geographic

        location, 147

    make light do anything

        you want, 147

light meters, 207

    illustration of internal workings, 185

    performance, test, 213

SEI (Salford Electrical Instruments)

    meter

        photograph, 184

light writing, 1, 147, 184, 219

Linhof, 1, 3, 94, 121, 208

    multiple exposure of Chinese figure

        photograph, 122–123

    self-portraits, 117

    Technika, 97

Lisbon Maritime Museum

    model shipbuilder scale replica of

        flagship *Apollo,* photograph, 163

    photograph, 162

    photo shoot, 163

London photo exhibit

    photograph, 109

LRH instructional critiques

    practical tips, 218

***L. Ron Hubbard: Images of a Lifetime—A
Photographic Biography,*** 5

L. Ron Hubbard photographs,
    see **photographs**

M

Mamiya

    C33, 153, 209

    RB67, 160, 208

***Mariana Maru* at twilight, China Sea**

    photograph, 28

**Marine Corps reconnaissance craft,
College Park Airfield, Washington,
DC**

    photograph, 38

Maspalomas lighthouse, 131

Mathieu, Matty, 220

Mayhew photo studio

darkroom apprenticeship with, 17

Mecablitz flash, 139

meters

SEI (Salford Electrical Instruments)
meter, 184, 186

Micro-Press, 82, 209

Mikvé Israel–Emanuel Synagogue,
Curaçao

photographs, 166–169

Minolta CLE, 191, 193, 208

Minox, 192, 208

Mission Earth

ten-volume series, *New York Times*
bestseller, 194

music

two-way communication and, 125

N

National Geographic

Guam photographs, 20

negatives

glass-backed, 117

skill of "reading," 212

ultrahigh humidity and, 43

New York Explorers Club

Alaska, 51

Santo Domingo photo shoot
of Christopher Columbus
monuments, 171

New York Institute of Photography, 79

Nikon, 208

F system, Nikon F3AF, 203

Nikonos, 135, 208

Norman castle at Tonbridge, England

photograph, 85

O

Old Brompton Road, London, England

photographs, 64, 68

Olympus, 207

OM system "Old Workhorse," 202

100, *see* Polaroid

originality

art and, 126

P

painting

two-way communication and, 125

Palo Blanco mining region,
Puerto Rico

photograph, 47

parish church, East Grinstead, England

photograph, 93

pastureland, Sussex, England

photograph, 216

Pentax, 145, 161

Auto 110, 209

ES, 160, 172, 209

6 × 7, 209

photographer

   attitude, 227

photographic testing board, 213

photographs

   Acropolis, Athens, 74–75

   aerial photography camera, Port Huron,
      Michigan, 36

   Alaska, 51–61

      en route to, 54–55

   Albania from the shores of
      Corfu, 181

   "Autumn Sky," southern England, 109

   beech grove, southern England, 84

   Bubba the Bull, Northern
      California, 199

   bullfight, 141

   Camp Parsons, Washington, 14–15

   Canary Island historical sites, 131–135

   candid of life in China, 29

   Canon, Athens, Greece, 72

   Capitol Building, Washington, DC, 12

   Caribbean Minister, 175

   "cathedral lighting effect" off Las Palmas,
      Grand Canary Island, 147

   Cedar of Lebanon, Saint Hill,
      England, 110

   China's Great Wall, 31

   church ruins, Santo Domingo,
      Dominican Republic, 171

   circus

      Sir Robert Fossett's, 104–107

   Citadelle Laferrière, Haiti, 1930, 38

   Creston, California, pastures, 200–201

   Crown Graphic, 66

   Curaçao

      Photo Shoot
         Organization, 154–155

   Doris Hamlin, 42–45

   double rainbow over harbor entrance to
      Kontokali, Corfu, Greece, 224

   Earls Court Road, London, 69

   eastern shores, Grand Canary
      Island, 134

   East Grinstead, England

      Jaguar XK 150 "camera car," 80–81

      outside, 84

      parish church, 93

   equestrian, East Grinstead, England, 111

   Experimental Aircraft, San Diego,
      California, 34–35

   flamenco dancers, 139

   flying bridge of research yacht,
      Apollo, 144

   formative years of Scientology, 65

   fox-hunting dogs, East Grinstead,
      England, 70–71

   fox hunt in Sussex, shot with a
      Rolleiflex, 112–113

   Funchal, island of Madeira, 142–143

   Gibraltar, 135

   Graflex

      Apollo, 3

      Saint Hill, England, 1

   Graphex

      Grand Canary Island, 130

   Great Wall of China, 31

   Greece, 72

   Guam, 16–27

Kensington, London, England, 62–63

Kodak Brownie Jr.

    Montana, 10–11

    San Diego, California, 8

Koni Rapid Omega

    Curaçao, 161

    Fort Charles, Port Royal,
        Jamaica, 156

landfall in Ketchikan, Alaska, 51

Langley Day air meet, Washington,
    DC, 40–41

lighthouse at Grand Canary Island, 131

Linhof

    Saint Hill grounds, viii

    view camera, Saint Hill
        grounds, 121

Lisbon Maritime Museum, 162

    model shipbuilder scale replica of
        flagship *Apollo*, 163

London photo exhibit, 109

low tide, near English coast, 108

Mamiya

    C33, 153

    RB67, Curaçao, 160

Mariana Maru at twilight, China
    Sea, 28

Marine Corps reconnaissance craft,
    College Park Airfield, Washington,
    DC, 38

Micro-Press, Brighton, England, 82

Mikvé Israel–Emanuel Synagogue,
    Curaçao, 166–169

multiple exposure of Chinese figure
    using the Linhof, 122–123

9th Nantes International Salon
    Exhibition selections, 109

Norman castle at Tonbridge,
    England, 85

nursery dahlias, southern
    England, 86

Old Brompton Road, London,
    England, 64, 68

Oporto, Portugal, 178

Parthenon, Athens, 72

pastureland, Sussex,
    England, 216

photographic testing board, 213

Photo Shoot Organization,
    Curaçao, 154–155

Polaroid Land Automatic 100, Saint
    Hill, England, 99

Puerto Rico

    abandoned mine shaft, 46

    Palo Blanco mining region, 47

    testing a sluicing chute, 48–49

Puget Sound, near Camp Parsons,
    Washington, 6

Queen Juliana Bridge in Willemstad,
    Curaçao, 172

railroad switching station, East
    Grinstead, England, 83

"real life" in supermarkets, Riverside
    County, California, 192

Rollei 35, aboard Chris Craft, North
    Africa, 146

Saint Anne's Church, Columbia,
    California, 194–195

Saint Hill grounds, East Grinstead,
    England, 76–77, 103

Saint Hill Manor, 78
    approaching, 220
    darkroom, 91
    long view of, 79
    photographic studio, 95
    using Rollei, 89
Saint Hill vistas, 79
self-portraits, 116–119
    Creston, California, 226
    rear screen projected
      backgrounds, 94–97
    using the Gandolfi, 151
seven turns of the Great Wall from
    above Nan-k'ou Pass, 32–33
silver birch, Sussex, England, 108
Sir Robert Fossett's Circus, 104–107
Southern California, 190
southern English countryside, 111
Spanish Photographic Holiday
    Shoot, 131–135
stereo-optic
    British Columbian anchorage, 50
    Native American village, 50
sunset from the deck of the *Apollo,* at
    Agadir, Morocco, 147
Sussex pastureland, 115
test chart, Saint Hill Manor,
    England, 212
testing a sluicing chute, Puerto
    Rico, 48–49
Tower of Belém, Lisbon, 148–149
Vasco da Gama flagship model, Lisbon
    harbor, 164

Voigtländer
    local riding academy, East
      Grinstead, England, 136
    Portugal, 163
volcanic countryside, Grand Canary
    Island, 133
Wang Po River, Shanghai, China, 30
Washington, DC's Langley Day air
    meet, 40–41
Washington Monument and Reflecting
    Pool, 13
Weir Wood Reservoir, East Grinstead,
    England, 103
Willemstad, Curaçao, 174
photography
acquiring skills of technical
    rendition, 219
action shooting, 141
aerial photography
    camera, 36
    Citadelle Laferrière, 38
    The Sportsman Pilot, 37
available light, 68
Boy Scout Photography Merit Badge, 9
camera stable data, 219, 223
definition, 1
difference between professional and
    amateur, 218
field photography
    challenge, 47
final codification of all
    fundamentals, 191
first frames, 9
instruction, 217

Linhof self-photograph, 3

LRH instructional critiques, practical tips, 218

mastery of fundamentals and equipment, 1

new photographic art form, 157

Polaroid Land Camera color shots, 3

"real life" candids

with Minox and Minolta CLE, 191

shooting wildlife, 198

stereo photography

illustration, 52–53

subject of message and, 217

technical rendition and communication, 217

William Taylor, study with, 14

Photo-Scenic Projector

1947 LRH invention, 95

Photo Shoot Organization, 157–161

cameras of, 160–161

twofold need, 157

photo shoots

Curaçao, 158

Lisbon Maritime Museum, 163

Mikvé Israel–Emanuel Synagogue, Curaçao, 167

Plaza de Toros, 136, 141

Santo Domingo, Dominican Republic, 171

Sir Robert Fossett's Circus, 104

Plaza de Toros

photo shoot, 136, 141

Polaroid, 207

back, 99

Land Automatic 100, 98–102

Land Camera, 3

testing of, 65

portraits

camera of choice, 65

self-portraits

glass-backed negatives and, 117

infrared shutter release and, 118

large film sheets and, 117

pneumatic cable release and, 117

ports of call

photographic vistas, 145

Professor Land

letter to, 100–102

Puerto Rican Mineralogical Expedition, 47

Puerto Rico

mineralogical survey, 1

Puget Sound, near Camp Parsons, Washington

photograph, 6–7

Purification Rundown

poster, 191

Q

Queen Juliana Bridge in Willemstad, Curaçao

photograph, 172

R

railroad switching station, East Grinstead, England

photograph, 83

"real life" in supermarkets, Riverside County, California

photographs, 192

rear screen projection system

description, 95

illustration, 96

Reflex-Korelle, 65

Rock Creek Park, 37

Rollei, 104, 164

Rollei collection, 209

Rolleicord, 65, 101

Rolleiflex, 3, 89

Rollei 35, 146, 209

Ryan, T. Claude

Spirit of St. Louis

designer, 38

S

Saint Anne's Church, Columbia, California

photograph, 194–195

watercolor, 194

Saint Hill

rear screen projection system

description, 95

illustration, 96

vistas

photographs, 79

Saint Hill grounds

photograph, 76–77, 103

Saint Hill Manor

approaching

photograph, 220

darkroom, photographs of, 91

photograph, 78

long view of, 79

photographic studio, 95

Sargasso Sea, 43

Scientology

brochure "A Student Comes to Saint Hill"

ninety-seven sequenced shots, 87

formative years, 65

Purification Rundown, 191

training films, 191

SEI (Salford Electrical Instruments) meter, 184–187

Ansel Adams use of, 184

description, 184

Hubbard Method, 186

illustration of internal workings, 185

photographs, 184–187

self-portraits, 116–119

Creston, California, 226

using Gandolfi, 151

self-timer

Blurless Shutter Release, 101

seven turns of the Great Wall from above Nan-k'ou Pass

    photographs, 32–33

Shackleton, Ernest, 171

shutter, camera

    speeds, test, 213

Sinar F, 210

Sinar P, 210

Sir Robert Fossett's Circus, 104–107

    photo shoot, 104

    slide show presentation, 104

slide projectors, 210

slide show

    presentation to Sir Robert Fossett's Circus, 104

society photography

    Washington Herald, 37

Southern California

    photograph, 190

southern English countryside

    photograph, 111

Sportsman Pilot, The

    aerial photography, 37

stereo-optic

    British Columbian anchorage, photograph, 50

    images, 51

    Native American village, photograph, 50

stereo photography

    illustration, 52–53

strobe light

    output, test, 213

Study Technology

    development of, 79

    failing literacy rate and, 157

    too steep a study gradient, 82

Sussex pastureland

    photograph, 115

Synagogue of Mikvé Israel–Emanuel, Curaçao, 167–169

T

technical rendition

    acquiring skills of, 219

telephoto lens, 89, 204

telescope

    Criterion 4000, 210

testing a sluicing chute, Puerto Rico

    photograph, 48–49

tests

    analyzing grain particles in film, 213

    analyzing test results

        skill of "reading" negatives, 212

    camera shutter speeds, 213

    color reproduction, 213

    equipment and film tests conducted in combination, 213

    film contrast, 213

    film sensitivity to light, 212

    flawless performance of each component and, 212

    lens performance and clarity, 213

    light meter performance, 213

new film fully tested, 212

strobe light output, 213

test chart, 212

testing board, 213

35mm systems

examined and tested all, 203

twin-lens, 89, 153, 164

200mm (long range) lens, 141

two-way communication

painting, music and, 125

Underwood & Underwood

publication of China's Great Wall
shots, 31

**Vasco da Gama flagship model, Lisbon
harbor**

photograph, 164

Voigtländer, 95, 96, 136, 145, 163, 207, 210

**volcanic countryside, Grand Canary
Island**

photograph, 133

Washington, DC's Langley Day air meet

photograph, 40–41

Washington Herald

society photography, 37

**Washington Monument and Reflecting
Pool**

photograph, 13

Way to Happiness, The

nonreligious moral code authored, 194

**Weir Wood Reservoir, East Grinstead,
England**

photograph, 103

"West Indies Whys and Whithers," 38

Willemstad, Curaçao

photograph, 174

THE
L. RON HUBBARD
SERIES

"To really know life," L. Ron Hubbard wrote, "you've got to be part of life. You must get down and look, you must get into the nooks and crannies of existence. You have to rub elbows with all kinds and types of men before you can finally establish what he is."

Through his long and extraordinary journey to the founding of Dianetics and Scientology, Ron did just that. From his adventurous youth in a rough and tumble American West to his far-flung trek across a still mysterious Asia; from his two-decade search for the very essence of life to the triumph of Dianetics and Scientology—such are the stories recounted in the L. Ron Hubbard Biographical Publications.

Drawn from his own archival collection, this is Ron's life as he himself saw it. With each volume of the series focusing upon a separate field of endeavor, here are the compelling facts, figures, anecdotes and photographs from a life like no other.

Indeed, here is the life of a man who lived at least twenty lives in the space of one.

FOR FURTHER INFORMATION VISIT
www.lronhubbard.org

The L. Ron Hubbard Series
A PROFILE

To order copies of *The L. Ron Hubbard Series*
or L. Ron Hubbard's Dianetics and
Scientology books and lectures, contact:

US AND INTERNATIONAL

BRIDGE PUBLICATIONS, INC.
5600 E. Olympic Blvd.
Commerce, California 90022 USA
www.bridgepub.com
Tel: (323) 888-6200
Toll-free: 1-800-722-1733

UNITED KINGDOM AND EUROPE

NEW ERA PUBLICATIONS
INTERNATIONAL ApS
Smedeland 20
2600 Glostrup, Denmark
www.newerapublications.com
Tel: (45) 33 73 66 66
Toll-free: 00-800-808-8-8008